Is God Who He Says He Is?

Ronald J. McCray

THE
Vision to Fruition
GROUP
PUBLISHING | INVESTING | CONSULTING | ACADEMY

Therefore if any man be in Christ, he is a new creature: old things are passed away; behold, all things are become new.

2 Corinthians 5:17

Ron During Praise and Worship

Is God Who He Says He Is?
Copyright © 2020 by Ronald J. McCray

Published in the USA by The Vision to Fruition Publishing House

ISBN 978-1-7339413-2-7
Library of Congress Control Number: 2020906791

Unless otherwise indicated, Scripture is taken from the King James Version of the Holy Bible, public domain.

Cover art designed by *Michael Ferguson*
Formatting & Design by *LCB Designs*
Editing by *Sylvia Hayes, of Covenant Consulting*
  Web: SylvSaidItFirst.com

Dedication

Heavenly Father, my heart is overwhelmed with gratitude every time I think of what You've done in my life. I remember the day You rescued me. On October 18th, 2009, You reached down and lifted me from a horrible pit and set my feet upon a rock—the solid rock of Christ Jesus. When I was a lost prodigal, You had Your eyes set upon me. I ran and ran, attempting to fill the void of Your love with many things and many people, but it never worked. I always came up short. You knew that one day I'd come to myself and realize there is something better for me at home in Your loving arms. You wouldn't allow me to go too far. Like Moses, when I was disowned and left to die, You were there and saved me. Like Joseph, when I was left in the pit, You lifted me. Like the prodigal son's father, You didn't write me off, but You received me and welcomed me home. Now, I am home to stay. You have blessed me beyond my wildest imagination. I only long to tell this story that You may be glorified and that the world will know what You have done for me, you will also do for someone else. Abba, I love you forever.

Fetima, my *boo thang*, my *baby,* you are my world! The love we share is incomparable to anything I've ever experienced in my life. You are truly my soul mate. You are the woman God designed just for me before the foundation of the world. I didn't know such a love existed. I treasure the ground you walk on and, I am honored to be your husband. It's you and I against the world. I'm so glad to know I don't have to do this thing called life alone. Let alone, with anyone other than you. I love you and I thank you for loving me when I found it hard to love myself. You spoke life into me and you didn't run away when others told you not to give us a chance because of my past. You saw beyond what they were willing to see and got something special, *lol*. Until the day we die, it's you and me.

To my parents: Dad, I wish you were here to witness the transformation God has made in my life. You and grandma, God rest her soul, always encouraged me to go to church, and I would not listen. But one day, I finally did and Jesus changed my life. Thank you for everything you've ever taught me and how hard you loved me. Sometimes, it was in a manner that was difficult to understand, but it was love nonetheless. As I always say, I am going to make you proud. Give grandma a kiss for me up in heaven. Mom, thank you for loving me and raising me to know Jesus. Had I not been raised in the Church, I wouldn't have known God in the ways I knew Him as a child. I thank you for showing me the value of prayer and fasting. I have maintained those disciplines to this day and it's because of you. Thank you for not judging me. You reminded me that the ones who would judge me didn't have a heaven or a hell to put me in. No, you didn't agree with the way I lived my life, but you didn't stop loving me. I treasure you, and I pray God pours back into you all you poured into raising us four boys. Love you, mommy!

To my other 'Dad', godfather, friend, and mentor, when I came to the church almost ten years ago I knew you as just as a leader of the church. I was seeking God but didn't quite know how to find Him. You took me in, a young man you didn't know and showed me the love of Christ. You and your family loved me like I was your very own. I remember when you invited me over for holiday dinners with your family and friends. I was learning what it meant to be loved by a man who didn't want anything from me. You called me every day to check on me, talk with me, and give me a listening ear. You never probed me for information or forced me to change. You simply showed me the love of Christ and led me to the cross, where my life has been changed ever since. You will never understand how impactful your presence has been in my life since we met. You are the father I always needed. Thank you for everything. I love you and the Lawrence family! You all have an irreplaceable spot in my heart.

My children, born and unborn—You all are God's gift to your mother and I. You are truly miracles. Without God's supernatural power at work in me and your mother's life, you wouldn't be here. Our very existence as a family is hinged upon the validity of the resurrection of Jesus Christ. If He didn't rise from the dead, we would have wasted our lives serving a God who doesn't exist. I am grateful to know beyond a shadow of a doubt that Jesus did rise, to which we are all living examples of this fact. Abba loves us so much that He brought us all together to show forth His glory. We have prayed for you and over you. We've lost and we've been heartbroken along this journey, but God has answered our petition and now you are here. You have the privilege of carrying both the

McCray name and more importantly, the name of Jesus Christ. God's glory rests upon you and He is going to use you in ways you cannot imagine. You will be targeted by Satan, but know that you are covered by the blood of Jesus. No weapon formed against you shall prosper. Represent the family name well, babies. I love you so much. Finally,

> Have not I commanded thee? Be strong and of a good courage; be not afraid, neither be thou dismayed: for the LORD thy God is with thee whithersoever thou goest. Joshua 1:9.

Daddy loves you!

DISCLAIMER TO THE READERS

Terms used to describe gay identification (i.e. gay people, gay-identified people, or *the life)* are not meant to offend the LGBT+ community, nor are they meant as designations of Biblical reality. However, they are reflective of words used to describe Ronald's life and experiences when he identified as a gay man from 2004 to 2009.

Table of Contents

Foreword

> For I am not ashamed of the gospel of Christ: for it is the power of God unto salvation to every one that believeth. Romans 1:17.

When I think of Ronald J. McCray, that particular passage of scripture comes to mind. I have personally witnessed the transforming power of God in his life.

I watched Ronald continually come to the altar for prayer on Sunday mornings in our church. One Sunday, the Lord impressed on my heart that this young man was truly seeking a transforming relationship with Him. In addition, I was led to reach out to Ronald to encourage him in his journey. Through a relative of Ronald's, I obtained his contact information and permission to connect.

We began our journey with me simply encouraging him by saying, "Ronald, God wants to fill you with the Holy Ghost even more than you want to receive it. When you receive it, the first thing you will say is, 'That was easy'." Shortly thereafter, Ronald received the baptism of the Holy Ghost. He came to me smiling and said, "That was easy".

Over time, we have bonded as I sought to encourage Ronald in his walk with the Lord, always directing him to prayer and the Word of God for answers. He has developed into a consecrated servant of the Lord and dynamic preacher of God's Word. He has consistently sought to reach out to others who still identify within the community to encourage them to accept God's gift of salvation and deliverance.

I rejoiced in his marriage to Fetima and the arrival of baby Alex. God is so faithful. I am so honored and humbled to be a part of Ronald's life story. I can say that I have seen the transforming power of God in his life, and I am so happy that this book will touch so many lives with its powerful message.

Elder Richard M. Lawrence

Chapter One
The American Dream

Ron and Fetima

Like many in the Lesbian, Gay, Bisexual, and Transgender community, I used to ask myself *Can God change me?* More specifically, I wanted to know if He—God, The Creator of the Universe, possessing all power in heaven and in earth—could take away my attractions for the same sex. I prayed and prayed to that end asking God to remove these seemingly innate desires, but there was no change. I rehearsed *Can God change me?* in the secrecy of my thoughts, as I sat in participation engaged in a conversation among friends. The conversation took place early one Sunday morning, not long after my friends and I had returned from our night out at The Paradox, a Gay nightclub in Baltimore, MD. This was our typical routine: We partied from midnight until sunrise and came back to the house to crash, because we were too tired or too drunk to drive to our homes. I was the youngest of my crew and I didn't drive at the time so I was on the time schedule of whomever was to take me home.

I slept somewhat comfortably in a sleeping bag on the living room floor of my friend's apartment in Laurel, MD. The lucky ones got to the pillows and blankets in my friend's hallway closet first. Everyone else had one of the sleeping bags or just a sheet to keep them warm through the night. Once the closet was empty, you slept in your clothes – either on the floor or on his blue, leather couch, which stuck to your skin when the temperature became too warm in the apartment. Oh, the memories! These guys were family to me. Although we affectionately called one another "girl", I considered them as brothers. When those closest to me turned me away because of my sexual identity, these guys were there for me. They were my community. This time, there were between six and eight of us in the room. One of my friends opened the blinds of the living room window, and when he did, the sunlight pierced through the blinds and into my eyes. Somewhere between consciousness and sleep, I rolled over to protect my eyes but I fully awakened to the sound of laughter and conversation about all the fun we had just hours before at the club. One of "the girls" presented a question to the room pertaining to God in relation to our identities as gay men. "Is being gay a sin?", he asked. Perhaps the question was raised because it was Sunday morning and a few were debating on whether or not they were going to church. I hadn't been to a church in many years so I didn't volunteer to go with them. The Church didn't particularly have a good reputation on loving people like me so I figured I'd stay out of harm's way by not going. "Is being gay a sin?", he asked again. One friend made mention of the story of Sodom and Gomorrah. Another friend said he believed God was okay with his sexual identity. He didn't feel being gay was a sin, nor did he have to change himself for God to accept him. Another friend recounted the many times he tried to change himself—going from gay to straight—but had given up because it was just too hard. His sentiments of attempting to change himself resonated with me deeply. But personally, I believed acting upon same-sex attractions was a sin. I was a church boy, outside of God's will—knowing fully the error of my ways.

Although I only knew God from a surface perspective, I was aware of what the scriptures said about the way in which I lived my life. But for the sake of not offending anyone and not bringing condemnation upon myself, I remained quiet. The general consensus was being gay is not a sin. It's a part of who we are and there is no need to change who we are to be accepted by God. Interestingly enough, the majority of us were raised in Christian homes, knowing what the Bible says about men who sleep with men and women who sleep with women (Romans 1:26-27). Yet, somehow, in their eyes, being gay was okay with God. I understand the term 'gay' can be used to describe one's experiences in different contexts. For the sake of this scenario, 'gay' referred to identity. The consensus of our ideologies sounded much like our society today with respect to this topic. Sexuality, regardless of where one falls within its "spectrum", is God-given. "I am whatever I feel, and God made me this way." As much as this statement appealed to my emotions, I couldn't accept it as truth. I believed God's Word was the final authority, not what we think or feel. I was immediately convicted by this conversation and within a moment, I had considered the emptiness I felt in my heart, although my sin was gratifying to me physically and emotionally. The truth is, I wanted more out of life than how I was living it. I interjected into the conversation a hidden desire, deeply embedded within the four chambers my heart. The words, "I want the American dream" came running up from my heart and out of my lips before I could stop myself from uttering them. I said I wanted a house with a white picket fence around it, a double-door garage, two dogs, career success, happiness, a wife, and children.

An ex-boyfriend of mine once told me he loved me, as we laid in the backseat of his black Lexus. With his strong arms wrapped tightly around my waist, he asked, "Would you marry me if I proposed?" I became frozen like a deer in front of the headlights of an SUV barreling toward it. As good as his love felt to me, marriage with another man was unfathomable. I wanted to be married to a woman, someday. I believed a man and a woman in a monogamous relationship was God's design for marriage, not two members of the same sex. I suppose I just regarded the desire for a wife and children as just an outlandish dream being uttered from faithless lips, not knowing there is a God who knows our thoughts before they reach our minds and who hears the desires of our hearts without words.

I was a gay man. The reality of me having a wife was so far from anything I ever imagined possible. I reasoned that God couldn't change me and I tossed up the desire for the American dream – or at least the wife and family part of it, and the hope of the gospel that can change anyone – as a fleeting thought. For whatever reason, I had these attractions I did not ask for. I didn't wake up one morning and decide that I wanted to be attracted to men. It doesn't quite work that way. If you ask any gay-identified person if their attractions toward the same sex was a choice, they would tell you, "No." A friend once said, "If I could stop being gay, I would. Who would ask for this?"

He was likely referring to being the subject of homophobia in our society. Being gay was difficult. Sometimes it felt like I had to fight for my existence, to be accepted, and to be recognized as a member of humanity. People didn't see me for who I was. They didn't see me as a person created in God's image, deserving of dignity and respect. Instead, it felt as if they viewed me solely within the context of my sin. I felt, at times, like the scum of society. I remember the looks of disgust I'd get from people and the distasteful remarks. I remember being called horrible names like *fag* and *sissy* by strangers in public. I remember being physically and verbally assaulted, rejected, bullied, and almost becoming a victim of a hate crime. If God could change a gay person, I had not seen any examples. That is, until years later, God would shift the very foundations of my life and reveal Himself to me in a way that was undeniable.

He told me He'd make me the change I desired to see. Can God change a gay person's sexual attractions? This question is tied to a lot of heart ache and pain for many people who identity within the LGBT+ community. All you have to do is search 'pray the gay away' on YouTube. Many same-sex attracted people were promised a change in their attractions if they came to Jesus. Coming to Jesus, to many of us, meant we would become straight. It was almost as if the gospel was more about gay people becoming straight, than it was about being holy.

American poet, writer, and Hip-Hop artist, Jackie Hill-Perry, calls this "coming to Jesus" decision *The Heterosexual Gospel*. Arguably, I do believe the gospel has, can, and will result in a change of attractions for some. However, I believe everyone's experience is different. I would say my understanding of the gospel was similar. When gay people heard Christians talk about Jesus, they heard, "You need to be straight!", and not "You need to be saved!" There is a major difference. Many of those same-sex attracted people, who were hungry for God, found that their attractions remained, regardless of their efforts of change. As a result, many were damaged emotionally and spiritually because the promised change never came. Sadly, some have taken their lives. Same-sex attractions for many begin early in adolescence. In fact, since my earliest childhood memories, I've always remembered being attracted to men. I was attracted to females too and dated them, but although I liked girls, the pull inside me was stronger for males. One thing is certain, though, I didn't choose my sexual attraction. My sexual attraction chose me.

DEAR LGBT+ FRIEND:
I can understand how the word "change" in relation to your same-sex attraction or behavior could be a trigger for some traumatic memories of your attempts to re-orient your attractions through the Church, or conversion therapy. I ask that you keep reading. Do not close the book here.

Chapter Two
The Family Tree

Ron, Mom, and Brothers

Born to Ronald Lee McCray and Annette Dixon, I came into the world on June 17th, 1987. I was my father's only child, but my mother had me and my three brothers. A sigh of pity for my mother who had to raise four boys with no girls. As you can imagine, she had to be a tough woman. Momma kept us in check. She ruled her home with a sharp tongue and a black leather belt. Depending on how bad we were, we had to pick our own switch from the tree for a whooping. My legs haven't been the same since. I probably still have my scars of disobedience to this day. I'm kidding about the scars.

My mother, Annette, sacrificed so much to raise her four boys as a single parent. She was superwoman in my eyes. It was as if she carried the world on her shoulders and still managed to put food on the table for us and clothes on our backs. I learned a lot from my mom. Perhaps some things I shouldn't have, like femininity.

I lived with my mom and brothers for the majority of my youth. As a result, I picked up mannerisms from my mother. I became infatuated with her hair, make-up, and even her heels and clothing. Sometimes I'd dress up like a woman and prance around the house when no one was around. Being a woman seemed more desirable than being a man. I wouldn't go as far to say that I had gender dysphoria, but I did want to be a girl sometimes.

My mother and I had a pretty good relationship. There is an unexplainable bond shared between a mother and her child. However, many regard the time a woman spends carrying the child as a justification for the natural closeness. For months, Annette toiled with a growing baby inside her body, and in her ninth month, she endured such great pain to bring me into this world. A pain I will never understand.

My brothers and I had somewhat of an ordinary relationship with one another. However, being the middle child came with its challenges. Separated by four years of time between us, it was difficult at times to relate to them. Subsequently, I was closer to my first cousins who were closer to me in age.

Much of my internal conflict began in the home. I didn't have the best interactions with the people in it, often making me feel alone. Although we said we loved one another, our actions and the way in which we spoke to one another didn't reflect the love we professed. We laughed. We played. We fought, and we fussed. But I suppose that's all families to some extent. Even though we would fight like strangers on the street, if we ever got

Ron, His Twin Brothers and His First Cousins

into a real fight with someone else, we had each other's back for the most part. We did ordinary things that boys did. We watched WWE and wrestled, played outside, played video games, and stayed up late at night just having fun. And sometimes we did crazy things like jumping out of a second-story window of a house, onto a mattress. We rode around the neighborhood and through a cemetery on our bicycles, threw eggs at people's doors, knocked, and then ran. We were bad! My childhood was memorable, to say the least.

My father's name was Ronald Lee McCray. Certainly, I look a lot like my daddy. If you stood us side by side, you'd be convinced we were twins. Our heads were shaped similarly. Our jawlines, eyes, and facial structures were identical. The veins protruding from our hands and arms, along with our innate artistry and love for music, instruments, and singing were all the same. My father was a multi-talented man with many crafts. He was a handy man's handyman. Ron had his own contracting business among his many side hustles. Perhaps this is where my desire for entrepreneurship comes from. I watched him work hard to provide for me. I may not have had all the things I wanted coming up, but he strived to make sure I had everything I needed. Many of my friends in the neighborhood looked up to my dad. He was a cool dude, and a bit hood. He was from one of the roughest cities in Prince Georges County, Maryland. We were complete opposites. He was hard core and I was gentle. I think some of the clashes we got into were due to the fact that I wasn't the kind of boy he wanted me to be. Masculinity, as he introduced it to me, was a mystery. It was very hard to connect with it, because I didn't understand it. Just like the boys at school, I was very different from him. It's as if he spoke one language and I spoke another. Dad was a rough and tumble kind of guy. He forced me to play football. I hated it. He wanted to box with me as a means of playful banter. I didn't. When I got jumped by some boys on the way to school, he forced me to go back and fight them, and I had better not come home unless I won. In theory, he wanted to help develop me into a man who could defend himself. For that, I appreciated him, but, it just wasn't the way I wanted to be taught.

My daddy loved me with his whole heart and I loved him, too. I just had trouble receiving his love because he loved so hard and in a way I couldn't connect with. Our inability to relate created an emotional disconnection between the two of us. The disconnection caused me to question if something was wrong with me. I didn't feel like I was enough as a child, as a male. I needed my father to speak identity into who I was. Yet, he couldn't. Affirmation wasn't a strong suit of my dad's, thus, birthing a hunger for masculinity in me. It was even hard to grasp the concept of God being my Father because I didn't have a healthy connection with my earthly father.

Although they lived in separate homes at times, my parents both raised me in the Church. There was a bit of a tug-of-war between whose church I'd attend on a given Sunday. My father was a member of Greater Mount Calvary Holiness Church in Northeast, Washington, DC. My mother's church was called Greater Morning Star Pentecostal Church (at the time), now Greater Morning Star Apostolic Ministries. I hated going to children's church sometimes with my dad. I didn't know anyone there, and I just didn't want to be there. He would drop me off and then go on to the main services in the building next door. I was a little anti-social and didn't want to be bothered with those kids. With the attitude I had, I needed some Jesus. I had a mouth on me that often got me into trouble. I actually enjoyed going to my mom's church though. I suppose it was because that is where the majority of my family attended.

There were two morning services, an 8 o'clock and an 11 o'clock. Everyone wanted to attend the first service to get out early and enjoy the rest of their Sunday. Mom's church was in the middle of an extremely narrow street. We were in the center of the 'hood and had to pray that our car would still be outside when service was over. We lived only three metro stops away from our church. Before we had a vehicle, our family took the metro to church every Sunday. We walked up the long hill from the train station to the church–hot or cold, sunshine or rain. It was worth it for me. I knew I could expect to see people I loved when I got there.

I often sat on the back row with my cousins, laughing, cracking jokes, and chewing bubble gum. That is, until the ushers caught us and made us spit out our gum into their white Michael Jackson gloves. You better not get caught chewing gum in the sanctuary. Those were the days!

I remember singing in the Youth for Christ choir and attending Vacation Bible School (VBS) during the summer. VBS is where I learned the books of the New Testament through a song my auntie taught to the class. Auntie is the matriarch of the family. She is a walking, talking, breathing Bible, in human form. No lie. She's a wealth of knowledge and wisdom. I loved going to her house as a kid because it was like Bible Study. My other aunts and uncles served in various ministries, like the Usher Board and Music Ministry.

My grandfather, the late Charles Dixon, Sr., led my maternal grandmother, the late Cora Dixon, to

Morning Star Pentecostal Church in March of 1966. This was after being witnessed to by a co-worker of his, who happened to be one of the Elders at the church. Grandma Cora responded in faith and obedience to the gospel message preached to her by repenting of her sins, being baptized in the name of the Lord Jesus Christ, and receiving the baptism of the Holy Ghost with the evidence of speaking in other tongues as the Spirit gave her utterance (Acts 2:38). My six aunts and uncles also shared this experience. One by one, God began to save our family and so I became 3rd generation Apostolic-Pentecostal. If you know anything about Pentecostal churches, they are known for exuberant praise and worship. It was common to see someone running around the church or sometimes falling out, speaking in an unknown tongue. It was the experiences of seeing people filled with the Holy Spirit, being baptized in the name of Jesus, and hearing the Word of God preached with conviction and anointing that shaped my understanding of the Church, Jesus, and His gospel.

My paternal granny, the late Willie Lewis, was a phenomenal woman. Although she is no longer living, she will forever hold the crown of 'The Best Cook Known to Man'—at least to my stomach. Granny "Grams" loved me and affectionately called me her "boo-boo". She was married to my grandfather, Joseph, whom I never had an opportunity to meet, because he was deceased before I was born. Granddad Joseph is who I received my middle name from. Grams was a Baptist. I loved spending time with her, but I hated going with her to church, because everyone there was old. I just sat there and tried to fall asleep when I could, but she wouldn't let me.

My father's side of my family is full of gifted people. I loved seeing them at family gatherings. I grew up thinking some of my second cousins were aunts and uncles. That's how close we were. It was always a party when the family came together. My grandmother's sister was a Pentecostal preacher in the 1960's. I didn't find this out until I was 29. Apparently, she and her sisters would pray over us as children. My cousin Mary calls it "The Prayers of the Mothers". So I was covered on both sides of the family.

Faith and prayer were integral to who we were. When the wars waged within our family, my mom would pray and call on Jesus to fix things. Those prayers sometimes included fixing my father. My mother most definitely knew how to get a prayer through. Christian parents or guardians are the first examples of Christ children have. Before the Church has an opportunity to teach them Jesus, children are already observing and absorbing what they see in the home. I learned a lot from my momma's example. She wasn't perfect but she made sure we knew who Jesus was. Annette would purchase *Vogue* and *Ebony* magazines from the store to bring home. Next to her prayer spot at the far, right-hand corner of our old floral couch was a brown, straw basket full of magazines. During her prayer time, she would flip through the pages and call out to God the names of those she saw while in intercessory prayer. She showed me that prayer is not meant for one's selfish desires but also for others. She taught me not only can we talk to God in prayer, but He can talk back to us. She anointed our heads with oil and prayed over us before she tucked us in every night. Every morning before we went to school, she would do the same thing. She got fancy and put a cross of oil on our foreheads that would drip down our faces. Our faces may have been shining in oil—which probably confused the people around us—but we were anointed!

When I was in the fourth or fifth grade, we moved in with my Grandpa Charles to help care for him. It was a complete culture shock moving from Alexandria, VA to Capital Heights, MD. Virginia was very culturally diverse. I had White, Hispanic, Black, and Asian friends. I felt safe. We could probably leave our vehicle doors unlocked and not have to worry about the vehicle being stolen through the night. Capital Heights was completely different. It was like *The Fresh Prince of Bel-Air* moving from Bel-Air back to West Philly. I hope the imagery is enough to paint the picture. Moving into this new area, we lived around lots of teenagers who were older than me. They often hung out in the cul-de-sec in which we lived. They would drink and smoke and sit on the top of their cars while they blasted their music. My brothers and I were often bullied by them. I was afraid to come out of the house at times because they would call me names like "faggot", "sissy", and "gay." I had to sneak out the side door so they wouldn't see me. I had to open our side door—which was out of their view—quietly and run down the hill to the train station or to wherever I was going. I had so much anxiety. One of the neighborhood girls was one of my worst nightmares. Even if I fought her, I would've lost. She got in my face and threatened harm to me, and told me I was a faggot. She dared me to say something to her and she'd knock me out. She told my younger brother that he'd be a faggot just like me. I missed Virginia. 'Are all the things people say about me true?', I asked myself.

It was all way too much for a kid to handle. There was conflict outside and inside of the home. I often watched and overheard my parents argue with one another. I wondered if they would fight as much if I wasn't in the picture. I have witnessed the sheer frustration of being stuck with the other parent of the child who is not the spouse's. The only thing linking the two parties together is the life they have created. I wrestled with thoughts of harming myself. I figured taking my life would resolve their issues because I'd no longer be the link connecting them together. I just wanted a happy home, even if it meant eliminating my existence. I envied other kids whose mom and dad were together, happily. I wanted happiness, but also consistency. In particular, I wanted stability with my father's presence in my life.

My relationship with my father was very special to me, as is any son with his father. For many years, my father struggled with a drug and alcohol addiction. Not having dad there at times left me feeling abandoned, unwanted, unprotected, unloved, and rejected. I didn't feel worthy of his love or his time. He made promises of us spending time together but wouldn't show up when the time came. A lot of the time spent together was me alone in my room when I stayed with him for the weekend. The liquor bottle often received more quality time with him than I did. I watched him stumble in the house in the wee hours of the morning, either high or drunk. As I heard him opening the door around 2 o'clock in the morning, I went to the top of the stairs to greet him when he came inside. Stuttering in his speech, he would signal with his hands to go back to my room. Then he'd pass out on the couch for the night. I suppose he came in late so I wouldn't see him in those conditions. But as I began to age, I understood what was happening. Moreover, I understood more and more the impact his addictions were having on our relationship.

I remember he called early one Saturday morning. My mom answered, turned to me and said, "It's your father. He wants you to get ready so he can pick you up." My face lit up like it was Christmas time. After packing my bag, I sat by the window with utter joy and excitement, waiting for daddy to pull up in grandma's purple Volkswagen. But as the hours passed, he never came. We received a phone call later to say he wasn't coming. My heart was shattered. I cried and cried in heartache. Why didn't he love me? Was I not good enough for his love? In my eyes, men didn't have the best rep. They were inconsistent, untrustworthy, abusers of women, abusers of children, didn't keep their word, and they didn't treat women with dignity and respect. I often asked myself questions like, 'Why me? Why does this have to be my life? I didn't ask to come into this world.' The broken link between my father and I created a longing for male intimacy. It wasn't a sexual desire necessarily, but it was a desire for a man to fill the gap where my dad's love should have been. His affirmations. His protection. His embrace.

My family did their best to fill in the gaps that he left, but I wanted my daddy. As the years went by, dad eventually went to rehab. I don't remember exactly when, but I do remember when I noticed a change in his life. He began to pick me up more and be mentally and physically present in the times I spent with him. I was happy that he was taking steps to better his life, and ours. He also began attending church more often. Church seemed to be a

Ron and His Dad

place people went to get help. I've heard it said: the Church is a hospital. Perhaps, my dad was sick and in need of a physician. He showed me that there is a physician named Jesus who was able to help people in need. Our conversations started to have more substance and I began to open up and share things with him that I wouldn't have otherwise. We talked about sex and dating, college, family, and a little bit of everything else. Our relationship was blossoming. Although we didn't get along all the time, I was happy that our relationship was progressing.

When I was in the seventh grade, he was diagnosed with colon cancer. The only thing I knew about cancer was that people die when they get it. I thought to myself, '*breast cancer is the reason my grandmother is no longer here today.*' I was frightened. Was I going to lose my father? Although our relationship was not what I wanted it to be, I still loved him and I didn't want to lose him. The doctors were able to catch the progression of the cancer within enough time to have it surgically removed and preserve his life. This was a scary time for our family, watching dad go through this experience where he couldn't care for himself. We really had to come together to take care of him. I watched him drop beneath 100 pounds. He was literally skin and bones. Helping my father was a bonding experience that brought us closer together. His cancer scare seemed to open his eyes to the reality that he would not always be here. He became more intentional about showing me that he loved me.

I went to live with my dad when I was in middle school. This is when I found myself increasingly attracted to men, as I started going through puberty. Before I had an opportunity to learn what the purpose of sex was, my innocence was compromised by a close male relative whom I trusted.

I was pretty shy as a kid. My sensitive personality, timid nature and gentleness often made me a target for bullying by males and females. I remember watching a video that described homosexuality. I don't remember the title or all the details, but I think there seemed to be two personality types among the boys at home and in school. The first personality type was the rough and tumble type my father wanted me to be like. These boys expressed their emotions through sports like football, basketball, soccer, wrestling, and other physical contact activities. The other personality type was the sensitive kind. They were the boys who were more in touch with their emotions and expressed themselves—through music, drama, poetry and theater, to name a few—much differently than the rough and tumble guys. I was the sensitive personality type who often found it difficult to connect with the other boys who expressed themselves in a more physical manner. My inability to connect with the other boys caused me to question my own level of masculinity, and it caused others to question my masculinity as well. When I'd make attempts to hang out with the rough and tumble crowd, they'd make it known they didn't want me around. I was often called out of my name because I was different than they were. My parents named me Ronald Joseph McCray. But those around me began to name me "fag" and "sissy". The names I was called affected me psychologically, causing me to question my sexual identity. I didn't understand the gravity of sexuality at such a young age, but I did know what the terms gay and straight meant. I never wanted to be identified by others as gay. I watched how some of the guys and the girls made fun of the openly gay young man in my elementary school. It felt safer and more acceptable to be identified as straight, but I found myself relating to and connecting with females more so than with males. The girls welcomed me into their circles. Hanging out with them was non-confrontational for me. I naturally enjoyed spending time with my mother, aunts, and female cousins, so I felt safe with women in general. Women, in my eyes, were trustworthy. The woman didn't betray me. The man did. This was certainly something I couldn't share with my dad or anyone except my best friend at the time. He was openly gay.

When we first met, I was hesitant to speak much to him. I knew what everyone said about gay people. Full of assumptions and immaturity, I looked at him as what everyone says about people like him and avoided him. But he made the class laugh all the time. I couldn't help but laugh at the jokes he made as he sat at the table across from me. Eventually, I let my guard down and began engaging with him in conversation. We often got into trouble for talking and laughing while the math teacher was instructing. As we became friends, we became close like brothers. We talked all the time on the phone. I felt I could trust him with my secret. I was sure he would understand what I was feeling better than anyone else. I opened up to him and shared my secret attractions for men. This was the first time I heard the term *The Life* coined. He made being gay sound so cool. I wanted to know what all the hype was about secretly. I later met other gay and transgender people who I would become friends with. I have always been someone open to having all types of friends.

Although I was secretly attracted to men, I continued to date women. I had a few girlfriends and came pretty close to losing my virginity, but it never happened. I couldn't deny it though. My curiosity about what it would be like to be with a man was running rampant. In particular, gym class made things really difficult for me. My eyes lingered in places they shouldn't have. My friend and I talked about the crushes I had, and I became involved in things my parents wouldn't approve of. I started drinking alcohol and smoking weed in my freshman year of high school. I began skipping school almost every day. No one at home ever knew—until I had to tell my parents I failed the ninth grade. I failed because I hardly went to class. With everything going on in my life, I just wasn't focused on school. I was thinking about exploring sexuality. All the kids in school were doing it, but I was unsure if I wanted my first time to be with a man or with a woman. I was confused. The more I talked with my friend about my desires, the more I became open to the idea of giving it try. And one day, the right opportunity presented itself.

Chapter Three
The Life

Ron In the Life

Before there was a *Facebook*, *Instagram*, or a *Snap*, there was *MySpace* and *Black Planet*. Millennials know what I am talking about. Being behind a computer screen allowed me to discreetly live out my fantasies of being with men. I was enticed by the idea of being with a man but I couldn't bring myself to actively live it out in real life. So I secretly cruised the profiles of attractive guys online. I roamed the internet while everyone was asleep. I told my best friend that I was going to experiment with being gay—which meant engaging in same-sex relationships exclusively—for a few months and then go back to heterosexual relationships afterward. I told him it would just be a phase. I was convinced that I was missing out on something by not acting upon how I was feeling. Although I believed it was wrong, it felt like the right thing to do. At least that's what my feelings told me. I met a guy on Black Planet who had an interest in me. He was very persistent in getting a response from me. Eventually, I gave in to his invitation. He and I talked day and night online and sometimes by phone. My parents figured he was just another friend of mine. We decided to meet one day on the green line of the Metrorail at Columbia Heights station in Southeast, Washington, DC. I secretly left school early to meet him. I walked about a mile to the station. When I arrived, I walked down the escalator to wait for his train to arrive on the exit side of the gate. A train pulled up and came to a stop. I scanned every passenger who got off the train but didn't see him. I waited a few minutes for the next train to come and there he was. I entered the gate and came down the escalator to meet him. We hopped on his train before the doors closed and rode the train back and forth from one end of the line to the other. There were twenty-one stops in total, probably taking a little over an hour to get to the opposite end of the line. My heart literally beat out of my chest every time he looked at me. He was so attractive and I couldn't believe I was actually living out the desires that lived in my head with another man. We talked and laughed the whole way. We sat side-by-side in the back of the train behind a divider.

Whenever someone got on the train, we moved away from each other so no one knew we were together, and as soon as they got off, we came close again. I didn't want the day to end. It was approaching the time school ended so I had to get off the train the next time it reached my stop. At some point on the way back to my train stop, it became clear what he wanted. Knees shaking and palms sweaty, I was ready when he decided to make his move. He leaned over and kissed me on the empty train with no one there to see what was happening. His kiss felt different than the lips of any woman I had ever kissed before. And in that moment, I knew being with a man was what I wanted. The kiss validated every feeling I had ever felt toward a man. It felt so natural. I guess you could say I was on the 'down low'. I was still trying to figure out my sexuality and my identity. I wasn't ready for the hatred from the world that came with being gay. I had no idea that one kiss would cause my six-month experiment to turn into a six-year experience.

We dated and became exclusive. He introduced me to so many other guys who I became friends with. There were plenty of people out there just like me. The relationship ran its course fairly quickly, but I made so many online friends who would later introduce me to what *the life* was all about. My next boyfriend, whom I met online, introduced me to gay culture – the clubs, the bars (although I was underage), the strip clubs, house parties, and the ballroom scene. He literally knew everyone. I wanted to find love, but the guys I dated were solely about fulfilling lust. I was sixteen years old when I lost my virginity. I would often sneak out the house late at night to hang out on the weekends at the Navy Yard in Washington, DC, where lots of gay men hung outside the clubs. I remember like it was yesterday. Sometimes you'd see people coming from behind the club or a dark alley together. I saw men dressed like women. It was definitely a new experience.

Being new to the scene came with a lot of attention. I quickly learned that if you were young, slim, attractive and stylish, you were in demand. That is, everyone wanted you. I still wore long t-shirts to my knees with baggy jeans. Everyone seemed so free to be themselves. It was like an underworld I didn't know existed. The style of LGBT+ people was so eccentric. Everyone just kind of danced to the beat of their own drum. This is what freedom looked like. People had the liberty to be whomever they desired to be in this community and everyone loved them for it. Everyone made me feel like I belonged. Who doesn't want to feel like they belong? As a kid, I often felt rejected by those who were supposed to love me. Receiving this love and attention was exhilarating, addictive even.

I later met a guy online who was raised in the same church as I was. Initially, I was shocked when he told me that we were raised in the same church.

Needless to say, we clicked. I couldn't seem to remember him growing up in church to save my life. He was older than me by maybe ten years. But I knew he was telling the truth about being raised in the same church by his description of many of its leaders. Our conversations about church made me feel safe with him, but they also convicted me at the same time. We both acknowledged that what we were doing was a sin, but by then, I was already too deep into *the life* to stop. We eventually took our talks from on the phone to in person. I caught the bus to meet him at his parent's apartment in Maryland.

When I arrived, we sat on the couch, watched television and cracked jokes with one another. One thing led to another and he began to make his move. I was nervous, but I didn't fight it. That is, until he became forceful and would not take no for an answer. What was happening? I tried to resist him, telling him I wasn't ready. But he used his strength to hold me down. There I was in the moment, realizing I was being raped. He told me I was weak and continued to belittle me. The only thing I could do was allow him to finish what he started. Afterwards, I put my clothes on. I didn't know if I should run or just play it cool and leave. I decided to play it cool and sit on the couch for a bit. Shortly after, I made my way out the door to catch the next bus home. He cut off all communication with me as if I never existed. I ran into him years later on the metro and he looked through me like he didn't see or know me. Why wasn't this experience enough for me to leave men alone and leave *the life* altogether? This should have been the end of my experimentation, but I guess it's easy to give yourself away to things and people when you don't know your value. I had been abused so many times before, and this was a continuation of the patterns of my life. Just like the other experiences, I simply pushed it to the back of my mind as if it never happened.

Still young, attractive, and in demand, I continued meeting other guys of interest. Six months turned into a year, a year into two. Eventually, I fully embraced a homosexual identity. There was no sense in hiding who I was anymore. This was the new me. I never imagined being married to a man. Gay marriage wasn't even recognized as an institution at that time. But even if it was, I don't think I could've gone that far. I did, however, want to be loved by a man. And sometimes I thought I had found love. However, for one reason or another, the relationships never lasted very long. Once lust was fulfilled, it was on to the next one.

My understanding of love was me giving my body away. The more of myself I gave, the more of myself

I lost. I had become addicted to sex. I was in and out of vehicles looking for the next high. Sex was the hit I needed to convince myself that I am worth something to someone, even if it was just for a few moments. I felt wanted for however long the encounter lasted. From one man to the next, I held on to the hope that I'd find love that would satisfy the emptiness I was feeling inside. I couldn't deny the void I felt within. But I couldn't explain it. The clubs, the parties, the men—none of it could fulfill me in the way I longed for. My heart was crying out for something deeper than the shallow experiences of the one-night stands, something more consistent than the frequent relationship changes, and something of more value than the desire of being wanted by men I didn't know. My life was spiraling out of control. The 'freedom' I had come to know came at the expense of my purity and my joy. I was so deceived. I had begun doing things I said I'd never do and going places I said I'd never go. I was tested for HIV often because of how reckless I lived. I was confident I would be positive each time I was tested. Yet, for some reason, I was negative each time. Maybe it was luck or a chance that the stars aligned so that none of the men I had been with carried the virus. I knew of some people who contracted the disease after their first experience. But yet, I never contracted it. It was like playing

Russian roulette with my life. After I'd get the negative test, I'd go right back doing the same things. I couldn't stop even if I wanted to. There was a gnawing pit of emptiness inside me. And I saw it in the people of *the life*, too. We all wanted the same thing. We wanted to be loved. But I found that what I was looking for, *the life* didn't have to offer me.

I had my induction into *the life* and now my eyes were opened to the truth. *The life* was full of empty, joyless, and broken people. It was far from the glitz and glam, wholesome facade portrayed in media. It was anything but that for me and many others. It is full of lust, promiscuity, infidelity, the nightlife, and pride—the deceptive pride that comes from thinking you can find true joy and contentment living your life outside of God's will. The kind of pride that says you can live life without any limits, as if there isn't a God who created our bodies for His purpose. My body was made to be the temple for the Holy Ghost to dwell in, for communion with Him—not for me use it for sinful pleasure. While I was so called 'living it up', I was dying inside. I needed help, but I didn't know I could ask for it. I didn't think God wanted anything to do with a sinner like me. I did my best to keep this secret life from my family. I did well at hiding my double life from everyone except my grandmother Willie. Apparently, she caught wind of the guy I had been dating.

I spent a lot of time with her, as I lived with her for a brief period of my young adult life. She casually roped me into the conversation about my identity and I eventually told her the truth about my sexuality. To my surprise, she didn't judge me. I respected her for not being evasive and respecting my privacy. One day, as we sat on the sofa watching television, she looked over at me and said,

"Rara, you need to find a church home."

Rara, pronounced Rah-Rah, is my family nickname. I told her I would someday. But I really just let it go in one ear and out of the other. She saw my need for Jesus. Mothers and grandmothers seem to have the sixth sense about everything. I think God gifted them with intuition. Some of my friends had come out to their parents, but I couldn't fathom how the conversation of me coming out to my parents would go. One of my younger brothers just so happened to catch me with one of my boyfriends in a very revealing manner that left no room for doubt that I was gay. So I didn't have to 'come out' per se, because he told the family for me.

One morning, my mom was up preparing breakfast for the house. It was just me and her in the kitchen. While I sat at the table, we engaged in conversation about something I can't remember. The conversation shifted, and I found myself confronted with something I wasn't ready to address.

"Your father thinks you are gay, because you spend a lot of time with your friend. He plans to ask you himself. Are you gay?", she asked.

My heart dropped into my lap. I thought I was doing a good job of hiding this relationship from my parents. I met my boyfriend at the bottom of the hill of the street we lived on whenever he came to get me, so they wouldn't see him. But I was terribly wrong. In the utter shock of the moment, I asked myself, 'Should I tell her the truth or lie?' I didn't have enough time to weigh the pros and cons in my head. I couldn't find a reason why I shouldn't tell her at this point. Heck, I was almost legal. Why not? If they put me out, I could find somewhere else to live. I knew my mother's Biblical views concerning homosexuality. It's abominable. But would she choose to love me and still embrace me as her son, or would she respond as my best friend's mom who put him out of the house and abandoned him? It just came out,

"Yes, mom. I am gay."

I sat in disbelief that those words came from my mouth toward my mother. What on earth was I thinking? Too late now. It's out there. In many words, she expressed her disapproval of my sexuality. Homosexuality was considered the cardinal sin in the Black community and in the Church. You can be a drunkard, drug addict, womanizer, but my

God, just don't be gay. She was angry! She immediately assumed I had HIV. She told me I couldn't eat from their silverware anymore (as if the disease could be passed on by eating after someone using the same utensils). The same mother—whom I cherished and loved to no end—in one moment hurt me beyond words could be expressed. I wasn't hurt that she stood on what the Word of God says. It would have been unfair of me to be upset with my mom because she didn't approve of something that was in contradiction to her faith. Nevertheless, I was hurt by the way in which she responded to me. This was the exact reason why I had kept my sexual identity from them. I explained to her that I was HIV negative.

Hurt and no longer interested in the conversation, I stormed out of the kitchen and ran upstairs to my father's room and outed myself to him as well. At this time, we all lived under the same roof. I figured I'd beat him to the punch. Surprisingly, he had a gentle response. He told me he loved me but wanted me to know how I was living was sinful. Fair enough. My father was black and white with no filter. Whatever he felt, he said, and he didn't care what you thought about it. I expected worse. From that day forward, it was hard to constantly be in their house knowing I had disappointed them.

I didn't break up with my boyfriend. It was actually somewhat of a relief because I didn't have to hide it anymore. However, I did have something to prove to my mother. I wanted my mom to know not every gay person is infected with HIV. I went back to the clinic at Prince George's Hospital Center in Cheverly, Maryland, to receive the negative test result, so I could prove my mother wrong about me, about us. I took the yellow copy of the paper from the clinic showing my negative status, went home, and slammed it on the table in the kitchen as my mom was washing the dishes. I walked away without saying a word.

When the news about my sexual identity got around, I was no longer welcome at the homes of certain family members. Many of my heterosexual friends ended their relationships with me also. A very hurtful rumor about me even spread around the family, and I was put out of my home. The LGBT+ community was right there, ready and willing to embrace me. My heart became like a stone toward my family. The ones who were supposed to love me hurt me very deeply.

Chapter Four
#MenToo

In our society, the conversation about people affected by sexual assault is primarily associated with women. The #MeToo[1] movement has relentlessly shined a light on the abuse suffered by women and young girls, especially at the hands of powerful, high-profile aggressors. But as we have learned through some who have become vocal about their experiences of sexual abuse in Hollywood, women aren't the only victims. Men are impacted as well.

In fact, according to the Rape, Abuse & Incest National Network, about 3% of American men or 1 in 33 have experienced an attempted or completed rape in their lifetime.[2] It's not easy for any person to share their experience(s) of being exposed to sexual misconduct. It surely wasn't easy for me. I lived in the shame and shadows of my abuse for thirteen years, in fear that if I told someone, they wouldn't believe me—or, maybe they would think it was my fault. I am not sharing my experiences of abuse as a means to say all people who experience same-sex attractions (SSA) are victims of sexual abuse. I know

---

1   The 'me too' movement was founded in 2006 to help survivors of sexual violence find pathways to healing. Available online at: www.metoomvmt.org

2Available online at: https://www.rainn.org/statistics/victims-sexual-violence

many people who experience SSA but were never touched in an inappropriate manner. However, this is my experience.

I vividly remember sitting in the living room with a relative of mine, as he and I watched television. As we sat, there was a tap on the glass-sliding door. It was his two friends. They came in, one of them carrying a black tape in his hand. He popped the tape into one of those old tube TV's with a built-in VCR and pressed play. It was lights, camera, and action. In that moment, a whole new world was opened to me full of lust and

Ron Age 9

perversion. I watched an adult man have sex with a woman. I was only nine years old at the time. I witnessed things no child should ever have knowledge of. I was extremely uncomfortable, yet intrigued at the same time. On one hand, I was repulsed by what I was seeing. It made me cringe. For all I knew, this is what grown-ups do. But on the other hand, my body became aroused with curiosity.

I soon learned that they had other plans in mind rather than just to watch the video, as I had become the object of their curiosity. They practiced on me what they saw the men do to the women in the flick. I laid there, feeling as if something was being taken from me. In my heart, I knew what was happening to me was wrong. I remember feeling like there was a cloud of guilt and shame hovering over me.

After it was over, I felt so dirty. I dismissed myself to the rest room to wash myself, but no matter how much I washed my body, I couldn't wash away what I felt inside. I began asking God to forgive me for what I had done. I believed it was my fault because I let it happen and in some ways, enjoyed it. Sexual molestation was my first sexual encounter and my first point of sexual reference. They told me not to tell anyone what we did. It was our little secret—a secret that would eat away at me for years to come. The abuse continued. Sometimes it was just one of them experimenting on me, at other times two of them took their turn, and at other times, all three of them had their part, making me to do different inappropriate things.

The tape continued to roll in my mind, even after we turned off the television. I can't remember the number of times this happened to me. Pornography was the gateway that introduced me to sexual, relational, and emotional brokenness. I began viewing myself as a sexual object, not an innocent child. I began to sexualize other boys in my thoughts following these experiences and I began to act out sexually. While I wish my experience of sexual abuse ended with the three of them, it didn't. It was just the beginning.

I was taken advantage of by an older teen in the neighborhood my family and I lived in when I was preparing to graduate from elementary school. I didn't regard the initial encounters as abuse when they happened, because I felt safe. One of my offenders was someone whom I looked to for protection. If I should've been safe around anyone, it should've been him. While I wanted to open my mouth and tell someone, I couldn't, because I was shackled by fear. I was told never to tell anyone about the things we did. There were other experiences of abuse at the hand of this family member, some of which are too painful to pen. I wanted to submerge the thoughts connected to

Just Ron

those dark experiences in my mind, as if they never happened. Looking back, I didn't have anyone I trusted enough to share this information with. I wish I had a safe space to tell someone what was happening to me. Life just went on with me carrying the baggage of those experiences.

I started working at fifteen-years-old. I was overjoyed to have my own money and a sense of independence. My first role on the job was learning to work the cash register. I advanced quickly and took on more roles, such as dish washing. I only remember two people from that job—my manager and the cook. The cook was an older man, likely in his 60's or even 70's. He spoke to me whenever I worked in the back during his shift. My dad often picked me up from work whenever I got off really late. He, too, loved the idea of me working and making my own money, which meant I had my hand out less for his.

One late night while I was washing the dishes in the back of the store, the older man walked passed me but he was uncomfortably close. Our interactions felt innocent up until this point. He was so close that his genitals grazed my butt when we passed by. I figured it was an accident, until it happened again. He began to look at me like he wanted something. The nature of his conversation with me became more about what I looked like without my clothes on. He was very unassuming. His initial sexual assaults toward me were very subtle. I remember becoming intimidated by him, because he was much taller than I was and was very manipulative in his speech toward me. He'd make a lewd comment toward me and follow it with a statement regarding my inability to handle what he was saying. He preyed on my innocence and vulnerability. I figured the manager wouldn't believe me if I told her, because I was a child and adults were always assumed to be right. So I didn't tell on him. I did my best to keep my responses to a minimum without telling him specifically what he wanted to know.

One late night, when I got off from work at 11 o'clock. I called my dad, hoping he would pick me up from work, but there was no answer. He had fallen asleep, which meant I had to walk home alone. I clocked out and began to make my way home through the rough, not-so-safe streets of Southeast, Washington, DC neighborhood we lived in before moving back to Maryland. As I began walking, I heard a vehicle behind me and saw the headlights giving illumination to the dimly lit street in front of me. The car pulled up next to me slowly. It was the cook. He offered to take me home, so that I "would get home safely." Hesitantly, I got into the vehicle, strapped my seat belt on and sat as closely to my side of the door as much as I could. I wasn't sure what was about to happen.

Our apartment wasn't far from where I worked. If need be, I'd jump out of the car and begin to run. He began asking me about my anatomy. I remained quiet, not answering his question. He said, "What's wrong? Are you afraid to talk about your p****?" But still, I refused to answer. We pulled up to my house, but he wouldn't unlock the door unless I gave him a hug. I leaned over hesitantly, hugged him and then the door unlocked. I ran into the apartment building door, into my apartment, and straight into my room and shut the door.

Just like the other experiences, I did my best to pretend like nothing happened. It wasn't long after this incident that I quit that job. It felt like I had a target on my back. For whatever reason, I was the one whom the predator and the molester came after.

DEAR READER WHO HAS EXPERIENCED SEXUAL ABUSE: *Pretending as if the abuse never occurred only cements the brokenness and dysfunction of your life. So many people keep their brokenness in safe haven by remaining in silence. In order to be free, we must be willing to go back in time to address what happened to us. It's never too late to tell someone what happened to you and allow Jesus into the hurt of your past. It's never too late to be free!*

I'd like to say no one would have ever known of the abuse I endured unless they were there. I couldn't be angry with my parents or my family. They had no idea what was going on. There was no one to blame except the parties involved. I was left angry, confused, and broken after what I had been through. I battled with depression and suicidal ideations as a result of the abuse done to me. I began to fear physical touch from other boys and men, especially those who were older than me. Touch, the one thing that has the power to heal, had been corrupted for me. The healing virtue exchanged through touch had been perverted and used to destroy me. I assumed every man had a hidden motive to harm me. The psychological damage from the abuse created a distrust for men. I often asked myself, 'Why me?' What had I done to deserve to be broken in the manner in which I had? So, I became angry with God. I was angry because He allowed what happened to happen. The sovereign God possessing all power, the God whom I believed to be in complete control of the universe, didn't stop me from being sexually victimized. I grew up hearing about how good God is. *God is good, all the time and all the time, God is good!* But I thought, 'If God is good, where was His goodness when I was being touched?'

Every time I was around the relative who inflicted the abuse on me, my body language shifted. The discomfort I felt when I was around him reminded me that he had hurt me—that he had taken something from me that I would never get back. I remember when my mother found out about the abuse. It was presented to her as if I consensually engaged in the sexual acts. Yet she had no idea how things really went down. The narrative was framed in an untruthful manner, leaving me to my worst fear— someone believing it was my fault. The brokenness which resulted from all of the sexual trauma shaped my identity as a teenager and later a young adult. At the age of 22, I opened up for the first time about the abuse. As difficult as it was to tell someone the details of what happened to me, it was necessary for my healing. Sharing was the beginning of my process of healing.

I wasn't looking for sympathy—I just needed someone to listen to me bare my heart—the area of my heart which had been broken for so long. But bringing the pain to the surface and removing the band aid helped me heal. A huge part of my healing process started with forgiving the relative who abused me at the age of nine. I wanted to have a face-to-face conversation with him—not by phone, e-mail, or text. I had to release him of his offenses. I never saw his two friends again after the abuse stopped and I will never be able to tell them how deeply they hurt me. But, I could forgive them and let it go from my heart. I could not move on in life until this chapter was finally over, and I closed the door by forgiving them. As I sat in the car next to him, my hands and knees trembled and my speech stuttered. I began to recount the things I remembered from my childhood. I poured my heart out about how deeply he wounded me.

"I feel like you ruined my life," I said.

I wasn't sure how he'd respond. Would he deny it? Would he become angry and defend himself? I was so used to him being abusive toward me, but I was willing to take the risk. I wouldn't know inner healing until we had this conversation. I said the words, "I forgive you", and the pain of what he did to me left my heart. He apologized sincerely for what he did, then leaned over, hugged me and wouldn't let go. He held me tight and asked me to forgive him again. The hostile feelings I had toward him left the vehicle when he got out at the end of our conversation. When he closed the passenger door, that chapter in my life was finally over. I was free to move forward in life, no longer bound by the memories of what happened to me. I am better today because I made the decision to forgive. It's true—forgiveness is not about the other person. It's about you.

Chapter Five
Relentless Love

It was 2006, I was in my senior year of high school just one month before graduation. My dad and I had been talking about post-graduation plans. Dad gave me two options: I'd either go into the military like he did, or I would go to college. My cap and gown had been delivered and I was ready to walk down the aisle to accept my high school diploma. A month before my big day, my father suddenly fell ill. He was taken to the hospital and passed away at 47 years young. It was as if my world crumbled when I lost him. Losing my father was like losing a part of myself. It was one of the hardest experiences of my life. I will always treasure the memories he and I shared. Every day that God gives me, I will strive to make him proud of the man I have become.

After his funeral, a man I had never seen before grabbed me by the hand and placed a silver medallion in it. On one side was a dove, and the other side read,

And by this we know that He abides in us, by the Spirit He has given us. 1 John 4:13.

I have held on to it ever since. After that day, I never saw the man again. My father's death caused me to reflect on my own mortality, even the times I contemplated suicide. When I had the knife prepared to puncture my wrist, and before I could swallow a handful of painkillers, I felt a resistance in my heart. This let me know it wasn't time to die. There was much to live for.

One of my outlets of releasing the pain in my life was my aunt. She is the youngest of my aunts and the one whom all my guy friends growing up had a crush on. At times, my dad was jealous of the relationship she and I shared. I could talk to her about anything under the sun. She was the big sister I never had. We talked about my boyfriends and the drama in my relationships. I saw the love of Christ demonstrated through how she loved me. She was a Christian who wasn't afraid to love me and meet me where I was. I never felt judged or pressured to change. She created a safe space for me to open my heart and pour out the pain that was in it. The conversation about Jesus came up organically between us, and at other times it didn't come up at all. Sometimes we feel the tendency to force Jesus into every conversation we have with our LGBT+ loved ones. It is perfectly okay to just sit and have coffee and talk about life. My auntie taught me a very valuable lesson: we can introduce Jesus to sinners by the way we treat them. The Christ she introduced to me, I wanted. The reality was, I needed Jesus. However, I didn't need someone constantly convicting me of my sin. I was already convicted by the way I lived my life. I couldn't escape it. The remorse for my sin would come up at the oddest of times—like when I was in bed with a guy I was dating at the time.

I remember having a conversation with him about giving my life to Christ and walking away from the homosexual lifestyle. As good as he made me feel, God's Word was whispering to me that the wages of my sin would be death. I could have a degree of happiness as a gay man, but it would never bring the joy only Christ could bring to a lost soul. Deep inside, I didn't want to be gay. Yet, I couldn't imagine what life would look like if I gave it up and would forsake everything I knew in exchange for a life I had not known in following Jesus. I had gained so much in my gay identity. I was loved by many, accepted in a community of people whom I could relate to, and I gained status. In all of this, I lost what was most valuable to me—my faith and the reverence I had for God. I lost close connections with family. While some may have distanced themselves from me, I pushed them away, too. In my rebellion, I wanted to get as far away from the Church as I could. I lost all attraction for women. I had no desire for them. What I had gained by choosing sin over Christ couldn't compare to the immeasurable blessings I'd have by saying 'yes' to Jesus and walking away from this life. But to walk away from my boyfriend at the time would have been far too difficult.

Still, I told him I couldn't do this anymore and encouraged him to seek God with me. He was sure that God was okay with the way we lived our lives. But I knew He wasn't. Trying to make homosexuality okay was like attempting to force God to change His mind about sin. I knew He wasn't going to do that for me or anyone else. His Word is forever settled in heaven and we don't have the authority to change it. Full of desire to please God, I ended the relationship. It hurt me to know that I hurt him in my decision to end our relationship. I loved him. I wanted him. But I wanted God more and I knew I couldn't have them both. Being gay and Christian was never a concept in my mind. That ideology meant I could still live sinfully and have a relationship with Jesus at the same time. If we look honestly at the scriptures, it's impossible to come to that conclusion. II Timothy 2:19 illuminates the truth. If we desire to follow Jesus, we must depart from iniquity. We can't have our cake and eat it, too. My knowledge of the Word wasn't enough though. I probably went two to three months of abstaining from sex with men and separating myself from the gay scene. But it was short lived. I needed power outside of myself to overcome my struggle with same-sex attraction. I needed the power of God. I hadn't heard the voice of God speak to me, but I did feel Him working in my heart. I knew at some point, I had to make a decision. Either I was going to continue to pursue love on my own terms or I was going to forsake this way of life for a life far more fulfilling than any man could ever offer me. The season of sin's pleasure in my life was running its course. The pleasure had turned into sorrow. It was hard to sin comfortably knowing I was offending God at the same time. I grew tired of dating different men only to have the same outcome. I grew tired of going to the clubs, the hook-ups, and the aimless pursuit of a soul mate of the same sex. It just wasn't working, and I was beginning to consider the fact that maybe it never would.

More than anything, I grew tired of being apart from God. I had lived all there was to this life. It was the same narrative every single time. I came, I saw, but in my naivety, I was the one conquered in the end. This experiment with sin had cost much more than I could afford to pay. It cost me my purity, my mental health, my faith, meaningful relationships – I was in debt to sin up to my neck. For the first time, I realized why I needed a savior. As a child, I knew God from a surface perspective – from other people's experiences and testimonies. I knew He came to be the savior of the world, but it wasn't until I needed saving that I realized my need for Him personally.

Chapter Six
No More Pride

It was Gay Pride in Washington, DC, in the summer of 2008. Pride, for me, was an opportunity to party, hang out with friends, and possibly meet a date. I marched with my friends in the parade but hid my face when the cameras came around. The nightlife was always poppin'. At the time, I lived in the basement of my mother's house. My friends came over around midnight so we could prepare for a night on the town. I saw a look of concern on my mother's face, as I prepared to head out the door. She asked me to stay home a few times. But I decided to go anyway.

As I got into the car and strapped on my seat belt, I saw a person wearing a white mask in the rear-view mirror, sticking their head up from behind a wooden fence. *Maybe I was tripping?* I hadn't had any drinks in my system yet and it was late. Maybe I was just tired. Within moments, the car was surrounded by three or four men with black attire and white masks. They had guns pointed toward us and demanded we get out the car and lay face down to the ground. I was paralyzed in fear. As I laid on the ground, the gunmen pointed his gun toward to the back of my head. He began to pat my pockets, searching for my wallet. I had forgotten my wallet in the house. I guess I wouldn't have gotten into the club anyway! I just knew that I was going to die that night. "This is about to be a homicide!", he said. I frantically hoped my mother would look out the window, see us, and call 9-1-1. But she didn't. Had I listened to her, we wouldn't have been in that situation. I didn't say a word. I just laid there as still as I could. I feared that if I moved, he would've shot my brains into the street. As little kids, mom taught us to pray and to plead the blood of Jesus if we were in trouble. I wasn't sure if God would hear me if I called upon Him. I had lived my life so contrary to His will and now—because I was facing death—I would call and He would answer?

I closed my eyes and began to pray silently in my mind. In that moment, it was as if I had forgotten I was being robbed. It felt like I was laid prostrate at the feet of Jesus pleading for my life. I knew that I would lift up my eyes in hell if the gunman pulled the trigger that night. I begged the Lord to have mercy on me. I promised Him that I'd give Him my life if He spared me. I can't tell you how long I was praying or how long I was on my face but I remember my friends standing over top of me, saying,

"Ron, get up! They're gone."

To my surprise, no one was killed or harmed. The only thing we lost that night were wallets and a set of keys. God demonstrated His love for me when He could have let me die. I was stunned. I couldn't believe I was alive. I learned that God wasn't looking for an opportunity to kill me because of my sins. He was interested in saving me. I was later able to comprehend 2 Peter 3:9, which says He isn't, "willing that any should perish, but that all should come to repentance."

Sometimes, He uses the things Satan means for evil as good. He doesn't expect us to come to repentance on our own, because we are unable to turn our hearts toward God without His help. His goodness leads us to repentance. Therefore, repentance is an act of God Himself, not that any man should boast in himself.

I saw God's heart for me clearly in this experience. God really did love me. God wanted me, and for the first time, I could clearly see this truth. I could not shake that experience. I promised God I would serve Him if He spared my life that night. But it didn't happen immediately. I still fought, but God still pursued after me. His love was relentless and unwilling to give up on me. His love was persistent. He was willing to jump through hoops just to win my heart and ultimately, win my soul. God is like a bounty hunter. He always gets His man. And now, He was on the hunt for me. He used messengers to be His hands and feet.

Ron In the Life

Not long after the robbery, I ran into one of the Deacon's wives from my church at the Target shopping center in Waldorf, MD. I had my days when I dressed like a 'queen', meaning like a flamboyant or a very effeminate gay man, and I had my days when I wanted to be 'trade'—meaning a masculine gay man whom you can't tell is gay. This happened to be one of those days when my jeans were as tight as my skin and my V-neck was to the bottom of my chest. I wasn't about to be caught in a conversation for her to judge me. You know how you see someone you know at the store, but before they see you, you move in the opposite direction without being noticed? Yeah. That was me. But I suppose God wanted her to see me. She said, "You are Annette's son. Ronald, right?" "Yes, ma'am.", I replied, with a smirked smile to cover my apprehension of talking to her. She put her arm around my waist and held me like I was her son. We began to walk and talk. She told me how happy she was to see me. I was waiting for her to tell me about my sin. But rather than addressing the obvious, she reached out and touched me with compassion. Not once did she mention my clothing, or the obvious fact that I was gay. Sometimes a simple demonstration of love can go much further than we think. Even if we never have an opportunity to bring up the gospel in conversation, a seed is planted in the heart of that person, making them ready to be watered by the person whom God will send next. Ultimately, God will give the increase. She didn't seem to be embarrassed by me whatsoever. While I don't recall every detail of the conversation we had, I do remember her telling me God loves me, that she loved me, and she invited me to come to church. The Apostle John tells us that love will be the identifier of Christ's disciples. This woman left an imprint on my soul in the shape of a heart through that experience. I could not say all Christians were hateful and homophobic. This woman had changed that narrative for me.

One thing I am sure of is someone was praying for me. God was in pursuit of me like a cop chasing a getaway car. At every turn, there was something or someone pointing me toward Christ—like the young lady I worked in the women's shoes department in Nordstrom. She approached me with a smile and said, "I remember you." I remembered her also, even by name. She is one of the daughters of an

Evangelist from the church I was raised in. It had been years since I had seen her or her sister. She taught me a lot about my job. We talked about church often and the importance of having a relationship with God. The conversations were non-confrontational. I felt really comfortable talking to her. She didn't make me feel like my need for Jesus was any greater than hers. The same God that could change her life was capable of changing mine as well. One night, at the end of our shift, we walked to the metro and took the same train to our separate stops. She turned to me and said,

"I may not be where I am supposed to be in my walk with God. Don't look at me as your example, but I want you to know God is a deliverer. He loves you."

Here again was someone else telling me that God loves me. 'Maybe I am redeemable', I thought to myself, and perhaps God really does love me. Every thought I had of God hating homosexuals was being dispelled by the people He sent to me. Why was God so concerned about winning my heart when there were so many others in the world who are serving Him? Why was I so important? I suppose Jesus leaving the ninety-nine for the one is nonsense until that one is you. God's love for sinners should provoke us in the same manner to love how He loves.

Chapter Seven
New Life

Looking back over the years, I have to admit I was a club head. I must've spent between sixty and seventy percent of my pay check on club entry fees, drinks, and outfits. Not only did Jesus save my soul, He saved my pockets as well. One night, my friends and I were preparing to head to the Dox. We had a few shots before going into the club, and we were 'turnt' all the way up! The club was packed as usual. The music was blasting, sweaty bodies were touching, and there were beaming lights piercing through the steam rising to the ceiling of the club. I was in my element. While I was out on the dance floor, I heard a voice say to me 'I have so much more for you.' I thought maybe I had reached a new level of drunkenness I had never been to before. I am hearing voices! "So much more?? What could be better than a life without limits? A life without some moral judge dictating the way you live your life? By society's definition, this was freedom. What could be better than a life uninhibited with the liberty to do with my mind and body as I willed? The freedom to love whomever I wanted and however I chose to. A life where I was my own god and lived life according to my own rules. In reality, this life I lived was a big lie.

It is a fantasy world for someone who lives as if God doesn't exist, and as if His Word isn't the final authority for all mankind, or worse yet, that He won't return to judge the world in righteousness and according to the deeds done with and in our bodies. The God who created the heavens and the earth was making a divine invitation for me to forsake all I had ever known for a life in covenant with Him, which was far greater than anything I could ever imagine. He wanted me to understand that I would gain more in Him than anything this world could ever offer me. All I had to do was surrender my life to Him. But to surrender would mean I had to surrender my gay identity. Moreover, I had to turn from everything God calls "sin" to a life He calls "holy".

Needless to say, I was challenged. Conviction began to eat away at my thoughts. We left the club around 6 o'clock in the morning. On our way home from the club, the sun was rising in the sky. I gazed out the window and into the fields along the beltway. I heard the voice speak those same words to me again. God was calling me out of darkness and into His marvelous light. All I knew was darkness, so the appeal to the light was enticing. I began having dreams of missing the Rapture. I would awaken from my sleep and call the relative in my family I knew would be caught away when the Lord returned. It's actually quite comical. If she didn't answer the phone, I figured I very well may have missed it. But I thank God He didn't give up on me and was willing to use whatever measures He could to bring me to repentance. Coming to Jesus required a U-turn in the opposite direction of the practice of sin, but I knew I couldn't walk away with my own ability. In Acts 1:8, Jesus tells us that when the Holy Ghost comes upon us, we "shall receive power". The power Jesus spoke of in this passage is the *Dunamis* power of the Holy Ghost. This power enables us to live above the dominion of our sin nature so we may live a life that is pleasing to Him. This power makes us witnesses to the world that Jesus is real and so is His power. He doesn't expect us to live holy and overcome sin of our own ability, but He helps us as we yield to the power of the Holy Spirit. If this power was able to redeem all, save all, and change all, then I needed to see it with my own eyes. I needed Him to prove His power in my life.

I moved into my first apartment with a friend in Suitland, MD when I was 20 years old. We were thick as thieves. We were like brothers. Just as any relationship between brothers, we didn't always get along or like each other—but we got over it. He was raised in the Pentecostal church as well and went to church every Sunday, routinely. He may have gone to the nightclub the night before, but on Sunday morning, he was in the house of the Lord. Meeting him was a blessing in disguise because he had a role in me coming to Christ. We became roommates under the following two conditions: (1) I'd pay half of the rent; and (2) I'd go to church with him every Sunday. I agreed, not thinking he'd actually hold me accountable to the church part. He had a calling on his life even though he was running from God. His nickname should've been Jonah. What was admirable is that although he was on the run from God, he wanted me to experience a relationship with Jesus that would transform my life. *The life* may have looked like glitter on the outside, but it surely wasn't gold.

He literally made me go to church with him every Sunday. I was a bit hesitant of going at first because I was very familiar with how unkind, unloving, and uncivil some who represent the Church can be toward people in the LGBT+ community. I expected condemnation. But my experience was far from what I thought. Everyone was so friendly. Unfortunately, all you see in the media about Christians in relation to gay people are Christians who go to Gay Pride Parades toting signs with hurtful, condemning slogans like "Turn or burn" or "God created Adam and Eve, not Adam and Steve", or even, "You are going to hell!" The problem with this type of rhetoric is that it does not communicate the gospel message. Jesus Himself, God in the flesh, said that He didn't come to condemn the world but that through Him the world might be saved. So, if Jesus didn't come to condemn, who or what gives us the authority to do so? The gospel is hope for the sin-sick soul that they can be redeemed from their sin and reconciled back unto God. This experience was almost shocking to me. 'Maybe Christians don't hate gay people', I thought. At his church, no one ever made me feel judged. It was amazing. His church played a role in changing my perception about the Church. Rather than ignorantly generalizing everyone, I learned not all Christians were the same. His pastor and their family really loved on me and made me feel welcome. Thank you, Greater Washington Deliverance Temple in Laurel, MD, for the role you played in God bringing me to where I am today. I love you all! I actually began to enjoy going to church at some point.

The experience I had at his church created a desire in my heart to return to the church I was raised in. I missed hearing the choir sing. I missed Sunday School. I missed seeing my family. I wasn't sure what to expect coming back. I didn't know if people would remember me, and I didn't know how they would look at me or treat me when they perceived that I was gay. But I still went despite all the reservations I had in my mind. I hoped to see the woman from church that I ran into at Target.

When I finally showed up, it warmed my heart to see my family's reaction of me at the church. I thought back to the conversation I had with my grandma Willie on her couch about going back to church, as well as conversations with my dad. He, too, wanted me to go to church. But I refused to go. I was now at the point where I was at the end of my rope and I was tired of running. Jesus had my full attention and I was finally ready to listen. Up until this point, I realize there was nothing anyone could say or do to cause me to turn from my sin. It was a decision I would have to make for myself. Moreover, it was something only God could do within my heart. I am grateful for a praying family who called out my name before God to rescue my soul from death and darkness.

DEAR READER: Don't stop praying for your son, daughter, niece, nephew, whomever. Sometimes it seems like when you pray, they only get worse. Just know that your prayers are reaching places your words to them cannot.

Although I previously wasn't in a position to hear some of my family talk to me about God, their prayers were effectual and reached heaven. And from heaven, God heard and pursued my heart until He captured it. Again, I was embraced with love. I began to go Sunday after Sunday, receiving the Word. My roommate came with me sometimes. We sat and listened to the Word together. Sometimes the Word was difficult to hear because it stepped on my big toe, the other three in between, and the pinky that hurts so badly when you stub it. I saw my sinfulness very clearly as my pastor brought forth the Word of God. I could do nothing to save myself. But I was convinced that through the death, burial, and resurrection of Jesus Christ alone, I could be saved.

The Word of God is powerful. It's sharper than any two-edged sword and it has the ability to cut to the deepest part of our nature—our soul and spirit. It is able to discern the very thoughts and intentions of our hearts. God was certainly doing some heart work on me and I could do nothing but respond in faith toward God. He was using the Word as a chisel to break down the stone around my heart. I would just sit in the congregation in tears as the choir sang of the goodness of God and while my pastor preached the Word under the power of God. The altar call, at the conclusion of the sermon, was a call to discipleship. An effective sermon should not be measured by how much you dance and clap your hands, but it should be measured by its ability to make you think and change. God was all up in my thoughts. I was beginning to consider that Jesus was worthy enough for me to forsake all to follow after Him. God was calling me for more than an acknowledgment of His worthiness. Through my heart and actions, God was calling for me to turn from sin and turn toward repentance. To walk away from this *life*, would be to walk away from the person I identified as for the past six years.

I could not imagine what life would look like being someone other than who I was. I was fully immersed in the gay life. I was going to be stripped of who I thought I was for an identity in the Lord Jesus Christ. What did that mean? Well, the only way I'd find out was if I obeyed Christ, picked up my own personal cross, and followed after Him. One Sunday, I got up from my seat and I went to the altar for prayer. Going to the altar was big for me. It was a response of faith to show God that I wanted Him. I was willing to walk down the aisle in front of over 1,000 people. I was nervous. But when you are desperate, you don't care who is watching or who you have to get through to touch the hem of His garment. I went seeking the Lord week after week. I was hungry for God. I wanted Jesus but needed help, I needed guidance. My aunt recommended I speak with one of the pastoral assistants of the church.

She recommended him to me because she believed he could help me. She asked if she could give him my number. I consented. I was very apprehensive because I didn't know him, but I met him after church and he seemed extremely nice. He called me that evening and introduced himself. He was confident he remembered me as a child growing up in that church, but I have a cousin whom people often mistake me for—which was the case here. He knew my family very well. He even knew my grandmother, the late Cora Dixon, who was one of the pillars of this particular church. God rest her soul. That certainly helped me to feel comfortable in our conversations. I was expecting him to immediately address my homosexual sin. To my surprise, he didn't. Instead, he made the effort to get to know me on a personal level. The focus of our conversations was about my need for a relationship with Jesus. Focusing on my sexual brokenness would've been like seeing a physician for having chills, but ignoring treating the flu—the patient's larger issue. A relationship with Jesus would right all of the wrongs in my life, and I would soon find that out. Parts of me didn't need Jesus—my whole life needed Jesus, not just my sexuality. I needed a reset.

Chapter Eight
Reset

I wanted so badly to start over in life. I wanted to undo some of the things I did and some of the decisions I made. I used to say I wanted to move to another state in hopes that things would be different. However, moving away wouldn't fix the pain and brokenness that lived within me. It would just follow me from state to state, and from this life to the grave. A wise woman once said, "Brokenness follows you wherever you go until you deal with it." That wise woman would later become my wife. What she was saying was, unless you deal with what is in your past, you will always toil with it in your present. For me, there were a number of things I needed to address. I used to lean on my pain as an excuse for the way I lived my life. I argued, "Well, if this didn't happen to me, I wouldn't be the way I am". But eventually, we have to move beyond the excuses. We don't have to live life as if there is no balm in Gilead. Karen Clark-Sheard's song, "Balm In Gilead" she reminds us, *"Jesus is a balm in Gilead. He's a healer."*

I tried to cope with sex, ungodly relationships, parties, and just doing life my own way. American analytic philosopher and Christian theologian, Dr. William Lane Craig, once said, "Life without God is meaningless". This statement is significant for those who don't believe in the existence of God and for those who do, yet live life as if He isn't real. It's one thing to acknowledge God's existence. But it's totally different when He abides within you and you give Him lordship over your life.

The manner in which I lived my life was as if God didn't exist. I ignored His moral law, tried to substitute Him with other men, and put them in a place within my heart where only He belonged. For years, I spent my life as a prisoner to lust, fornication, lies, rebellion, infidelity and ultimately, sin. The thrill of living *the life* was quickly losing its appeal to me. I was tired of crying the same tears from a broken heart. I needed a change. I needed Jesus to hit the reset button on my life. I wanted a new name and a new identity, whereby no one knew me for the sinful things I had done. I wanted to know if Jesus would be willing to cleanse me of all of my unrighteousness. Was the God of the Bible truly who He says He is? Could He cleanse me as He cleansed the leapers? I had already done so much, I thought that made me nonredeemable. But when I look through the scriptures, I read about imperfect, sinful men and women, whom Jesus chose to save and use in His kingdom. Jesus didn't come for the self-proclaimed righteous, or those who didn't think they needed Him. Instead, he came to call sinners to repentance—those who knew they needed saving. He came for the broken. He came for people like me. Jesus wasn't calling me to turn from being gay only. He was calling me to turn from the way I had lived my life without Him and make the choice to follow Him. Portions of Ronald didn't need to be redeemed, all of Ronald needed redemption. Homosexuality is just a leaf or a branch on the tree of sin.

I could have stopped dating men, denied myself of my same-sex attractions, started dating women, and would still be a sinner, worthy of death under God's righteous judgment. It's David who tells us that we were born into a sin nature that naturally rebels against God. But our redemption was purchased through the shedding of Jesus Christ's blood. His blood is the only means by which we can be saved and transformed from a sinner to a child of God.

So, it isn't a gay to straight thing, it's a lost to saved thing. It is the necessary transition from sin to a life in pursuit of holiness. Nailed to the cross on Golgotha's Hill were the sins every person born into this world would ever commit— including the sin of homosexuality. If Jesus didn't die and rise again on the third day, all of humanity would be lost and destined for hell. That, to me, was the greatest demonstration of love mankind will ever know. His death proved His love for sinners like me and His desire to have relationship with us broken, sinful people.

I knew I couldn't have both my sin and Christ at the same time. I had to make a choice as to the direction of my life. A part of repentance for me meant death to the same-sex relationships. As much as my flesh tried to justify its reasons to remain in *the life*, I could not find one scripture in the Bible that condoned it. I could not imagine what life would look like other than how I had lived it for the past six years as a homosexual man. I couldn't imagine being with a woman. Primarily, because I had no attraction to women or desire for them. Surely, no woman would want to be with a man who was once in relationships with other men. I figured I'd be single and celibate for the rest of my life. As daunting of the reality of lifelong celibacy was for me, I was willing to do it. But with all the reservations I had in my heart, I was ready to take Jesus by the hand and allow Him to lead my life. What did I have to lose? I had tried everything else. All along, God's kindness toward me and His mercy was leading me to this point and I didn't even know it. It was His loving kindness that drew me to His heart, not His wrath.

For the first time in God knows how long, I began to pray. My heart was becoming full of conviction through the sermons I heard preached at church. I asked God to help me live for Him because I knew I couldn't serve Him with my own strength. There was a war within my heart. It was the conflict between my desire to forsake my life for Christ or to pursue a relationship with the man I had such deep affections for. I would be taking a chance with my heart. Would a relationship with Jesus satisfy me more than he could? I suppose that's why they call it faith. I could not see the answers to my questions. Like Abraham, God was calling me to leave everything I once knew to follow Him to a new land, a new life.

The leader whom I connected with at my church and I continued talking over time. Our conversations were never narrowly about my sexuality. I found that my brokenness was more than my sexuality. I was broken at the core of who I was. I never felt pressured or forced to change. He created a safe environment for me and within that space, ministered God's love to me. I didn't go to a conversion therapy camp, nor did this church promise my salvation experience would take away my same-sex attractions and temptations. Rather, the focus was having a relationship with the King of the world. I finally expressed my desire to be saved. He pointed me to the scriptures. He showed me the Bible's prescriptive solution for mankind's sin problem. It didn't matter who you were, how you identified, or what your sin was. If we are going to be delivered from the bondage of our sin nature and escape God's judgment, we must be born again of both water and spirit (John 3:3). In the book of Acts, the Apostle Peter details what that looks like:

> *"Repent, and be baptized every one of you in the name of Jesus Christ for the remission of sins, and ye shall receive the gift of the Holy Ghost."* Acts 2:38

When we have repented and are baptized, the debt of sin is canceled because the blood of Jesus has been applied to us through our faith in Christ's sacrifice and obedience to the gospel. We are then, no longer under God's wrath, but forgiven. When we have repented, once we arise from the water, we can have confidence through God's Word that every sin we've ever committed has been forgiven. The power of the Holy Ghost enables us to say 'no' to sin, and empowers us to live a life above the rule of sin. My identity as a gay man would be no more. All of that would change, as I would be adopted into the family of God—making me His child.

It was Sunday, October 18th, 2009. Tired and likely hungover from the club the night before, I awoke the next day with a desire to go to church. Of all weekends, my roommate decided to stay home, but the thirst inside of me for God would not let me go back to sleep. I asked him if I could borrow his truck to go to church on my own and he agreed. I showered, got dressed, and headed out the door. I traveled up I-95 North to Upper Marlboro, MD. On the way there, I listened to gospel music to help center my mind on Jesus. I pulled up to the traffic light in front of the church as it turned red, bringing me to a complete stop. I remember glancing at the church out of the car window. I had decided that day would be the day I surrendered my life to Jesus and received His Spirit. As I sat during the service, the adult choir was singing before my pastor got up to preach. My eyes were flooded with tears as they sang. The presence of God rested upon me. It felt like He was pouring out His love over me. I began to recall my sinfulness and the kindness He had shown me. When God could have stood back and allowed death to swallow me up, He intervened and stopped death in its tracks. I cried and cried in my seat, pouring out my soul to God. Although my sin was great, His love for me was greater. My pastor took his position to preach his sermon, but before he did, two people had come up to the front to testify to the church. They shared with the church that they had received the gift of the Holy Spirit that day, which was inspiration to me. The church began to praise and worship God. As worship went forth, my heart was leaping, hoping to be filled myself. I recall my pastor saying,

"The Lord is still giving away the Holy Ghost! If you want it, come now!"

I got up and made my way down the aisle. I went into the tarry room, got down on my knees, and just began talking to Jesus silently in my mind. However, out of my mouth was,

"Thank you, Jesus!", over and over again.

The tears began falling from my face. Repentance was ripe in my heart. I began asking God to forgive me for every sinful thing that came to mind. As I called on His name, my speech began to change. I found myself speaking in a language I had never learned. I didn't have anyone standing over me, asking me to repeat after them. I wasn't repeating something I'd heard before. It was an authentic experience. The presence of God filled the room – and He filled me, too. Hallelujah! It was an experience unlike anything I had experienced in my life. I had received the baptism of the Holy Ghost – God's Spirit living inside of me. I was taught from the scriptures that the Holy Ghost gives us the power and ability to live in a manner pleasing to Him. I once felt like I had to clean myself up before I could come to God. The task seemed very difficult — in fact, it was impossible. It takes God to both clean us and keep us. I started coming to Bible Study to hear more about God's Word. In this 'anti-church', Christian generation we live in, I still highly recommend the Church. There is so much that we gain and benefit from by being in church among believers. It is irreplaceable.

At the end of service, I came out to testify before the congregation that I, too, had been filled with the gift of the Holy Ghost. After church was over, I hugged what felt like fifty million people on my way out the door. The love this church showed me has been etched in my heart. The Church is often generalized as gay bashers and homophobic bigots. While it may be true for some churches, that certainly was not the case for Greater Morning Star.

I drove to my mother's house after church was over and I knocked on the door, excited to see the expression on my mother's face when I told her the good news! She was elated! We both rejoiced and offered praise to God. My mom was about to see a transformation in the son who once identified as a gay man. Not only her, but everyone who knew me and my sexuality. I called the guy I was seeing and explained what just happened to me. His response wasn't surprising, as he was raised in a Pentecostal church as well. He told me he was happy for me. He understood. I let him know the nature of our relationship would have to change. Fortunately, we remained friends since then. I couldn't wait to share the news with my roommate when I got home. I wanted to tell the whole world! I went home, opened my Bible, and began to read. I must've read all day until I fell asleep. My roommate told me he had been praying for me, specifically that I would experience salvation. God heard his prayers and answered. I know that if He can do it for me, He can and will do it for anyone who is willing to accept Him on His terms.

As I learned more about this wonderful God who now lived inside of me, I became a student and lover of the Bible. My aunt gave me some sermons to listen to in order to develop my faith. Everything happened so quickly. I was literally in the club the previous weekend and filled with the Holy Spirit the following weekend. It was a sudden shock for my friends and family, and understandably so. The Ronald they once knew had died. I was a new creation. Although I may have looked the same on the outside, there was a wonderful change that had taken place in my heart and soul. I went back to work Monday morning a new man. My inner circle of friends and I talked every day via group e-mail all day long to help our work day go by faster. We talked about all types of things from our recent encounters, to other unmentionables. But this time, I had something new to share with them. I told them of my experience of receiving the baptism of the Holy Spirit just the day before. I expected support, especially from those who were churchgoers.

"Don't believe everything you hear," one replied.

Some didn't respond at all. Over time, one after the other, some laughed and mocked me. I didn't understand it, coming from people who professed to believe in God and His Word. It was evident from that day forward, the dynamic of our relationships were bound to be different. I no longer desired to engage in topics of conversation that would displease the Lord. It was tough because some of them were like brothers to me. Jesus didn't warn me about the fallout in my friendships when He called me to Himself.

There were some at work who told me there was something noticeably different about me. Of course, high on zeal, I seized the opportunity to tell them what Jesus had done. I became the office evangelist at work. I would be off in a corner of the call center, reading and explaining the scriptures to a group of my co-workers. Some of them came to church and were baptized. The Lord ignited a flame within me to be a witness for Him. Everyone already knew of my pre-salvation sexuality, at work and outside of work. So I wasn't embarrassed to tell people I had been delivered. Some didn't believe me and talked about me behind my back. 'Once gay, always gay!' Perhaps this was the first time they heard of someone being delivered. Still, I stood. However, sometimes I questioned if what they were saying was right. Was I just deceiving myself by suppressing feelings that came so naturally? I combated the lies Satan tried to tell me with the Word of God. My identity was no longer by the world's definition. It was everything God said about me in His Word.

Every time the doors of the church were opened, I was there. In addition to listening to the preachers and teachers within my church, I learned of a man named Reverend David K. Bernard of the United Pentecostal Church International. His online teachings and sermons were incredibly helpful in my understanding of the Word of God. I would still hang out with my friends from time to time, as they were the only friends I had. But when I went around them, I found myself acting out and saying things like I did before I knew Christ. I found myself speaking in gay lingo and feeling the tendency to exhibit feminine mannerisms. The Holy Spirit did a fine job of convicting me. The way I acted out around them did not agree with the Spirit that now lived within me. So immediately, the war between the flesh and the Spirit began. I knew He was telling me I needed to separate myself from them, but I just couldn't bear parting ways with the people who loved me and accepted me when others rejected me. Surely, I could hang around the same people and maintain my salvation.

Chapter Nine
You Can't Run with the Foxes
and Bark with the Hounds!

My pastor, Bishop Charles E. Johnson, often shares a quote from our former Pastor, the late Bishop Ramsey Nathaniel Butler,

"You can't run with the foxes and bark with the hounds".

It is a statement with great spiritual implication. I couldn't run with those whom I used to sin with, still finding pleasure in doing the things we used to do and still walk in my identity as a child of God. I was being stripped of everything I knew about myself—my associations, friend groups, how I presented myself—all so that He could make me into who he created me to be and to protect His investment in my soul. Sanctification is the process of separation from the world. After which you are born again, it is the means by which we are purified through the Spirit of God in our pursuit of holiness, and the process by which we are being saved. In my opinion, it is a life-long process that all of us must go through. It's a time where the Lord purges us of the filth of our old nature. God never intended for us to continue in the practice of sin once we have been redeemed from it. We no longer have the excuse of 'we all sin' as a license to commit sin. We now possess the power of the resurrection of Jesus Christ within us to help us overcome the dominion of sin that once controlled us. God has now set us apart for His purpose and for His good pleasure. We are now temples of the living God. Separation from my *brothers* was a huge challenge for me. I had been friends with some of them for many years and we had been through tough times in life together. Now God was asking me to separate myself from them and even sever friendships with some. My fear was they wouldn't understand the separation. I didn't fully understand it myself. What would I tell them is the reason for the change in our relationship? I didn't want them to perceive my change of identity as me assuming I was better than they are, because I wasn't. Being the visual learner that I am, God had to show me why He was bringing about the change. I learned the separation was more so about me than it was about them.

On one of those lonely Saturday nights when I had nothing to do, my home boy asked me if I wanted to go to the club with the crew. The Spirit was screaming 'No!', but deep down inside, I wanted to go because I didn't want to be lonely that night. My younger brother, also now in *the life*, happened to call me to let me know he'd also be at the club that night. He encouraged me not to go because he didn't think it was a good environment for me to be in, considering my new life in Christ. But my desire to preserve my fading relationships with my friends influenced me to still go. Not once, but twice. My flesh wanted so badly to have no conviction with going to the clubs and still maintain the same closeness with my gay friends. If conviction were a light switch, I would've turned it off until I got back home from the club so I could at least enjoy myself for the night. But Holy Spirit was like 'Nah, bruh! You need to get out of here!' With every dance move I made, conviction was all over me. I couldn't even enjoy myself anymore. I repented and I asked the Lord to help me not to go back. It just wasn't the same anymore. The music was the same. The same people were there, as always. However, internally there was something different. I was grieving the Holy Spirit by being in an environment that was not conducive for the enrichment of my soul. It would be a matter of time before I went back, had I not made the separation.

I just couldn't ignore the conviction any longer. On the ride home around 4 o'clock in the morning, I turned the music down and turned to my friends. I told them it would be my last time going out to the club. I told them I knew God was expecting more from me. You could have heard a pin drop in the car had one fallen. Honestly, I didn't expect them to know what to say. The person they had known for several years was suddenly someone completely different. They had to get to know the new me and to be honest, so did I. I didn't know what it meant to live a holy lifestyle or to be saved. I was learning. I didn't know what the next day would look like on this journey. I had to have the confidence that God knew what He was doing with my life and be willing to fully submit to Him. I knew that I had to be an example. If I wanted to win them to Christ, I had to demonstrate God to them through the way I lived my life, not merely by the words I said from my mouth. As our relationships changed, I went into a period of deep loneliness. My nights and weekends weren't spent at the parties anymore. I spent a lot of time in the house alone—in prayer, reading the Bible, and attempting to figure out my new life as a Christian. Although I was happy with my new life, the loneliness I felt sucked. One of the biggest fears I had before giving my life to Jesus was being alone. I wrestled with the urge to pick up the phone and call my friends so we could hang out. Sometimes, I had to fight the desire to call an old fling to come over just to hold me. I was delivered from the practice of homosexuality, but I had other issues to work through in my heart.

I had an addiction to porn and masturbation that I needed to divorce. Yes, it was sexually and emotionally stimulating, but in many ways, those addictions also satisfied the void of loneliness and intimacy inside me. I needed to allow God into the empty spaces so that my desire would not be to fill myself with my vices again, but to fill myself with Him. I was still attracted to men and even desired them sexually. I couldn't be with them physically, so porn was a way to hold on to the experience in my mind. I was too ashamed to tell anyone. I assumed people would question my salvation if I exposed my struggles. I even questioned whether or not I was delivered because my desires for men had not changed as I thought they would. As long as I engaged in pornography, my mind was in a constant state of bondage. I was tormented with sexual dreams every single day of the first year of my new life. Literally. I even had dreams where I had fallen into sexual sin and someone would be there to say 'Aren't you the one who said he's delivered? Look at you now!' The dreams felt like real life in every sense of the imagination. I would wake up feeling as if I had actually performed the acts in real life. The warfare was real. I would wake up in tears, only to realize it was just a dream. Demonic spirits were attacking me through the portal I had let them in through. They attacked me with accusations and with fear—the fear that I would fall back into sin. It was to the point where I felt presences in my apartment. I didn't know how to break free from this secret struggle until one day God spoke to me in prayer and gave me instruction.

> **DEAR READER: You can't overcome secret sins if you aren't willing to ask for help and expose yourself. Don't suffer in silence when you can be free.**

God told me to go to the book of Acts 16:16 in my Bible. He directed me here where Paul and Silas met the young lady possessed with a spirit of divination. Paul became vexed with the spirit and commanded it to come out of her by the power and authority that is in the name of Jesus. I walked throughout my apartment and rebuked the spirits by name. As I called them out, I could feel forces pushing against me. I am not telling a fictional story. As I stood in my bedroom, I commanded the spirits to leave in Jesus' name, and they left.

> **PRESS PAUSE MOMENT: There is authority in the name of Jesus. You don't have to be bullied by the devil. Rebuke him and he will flee!**

From that day forward, I did not have any more sexual dreams and my addiction to porn was broken. I still struggled with masturbation and it took some time for God to deliver me from it but I had not gone back to porn since. Not only had I been freed from the bondage of porn, God had taken away the images that constantly rotated in my mind. I mustered the courage to share that struggle with someone in leadership who could hold me accountable, as well as my pastor. Talking to my pastor was the best decision I could have ever made. Satan thrives off of secret struggles. He uses the fear of embarrassment to keep us from getting the help that is available to us. If he can keep our struggles private long enough, eventually we may fall into sin. It will cause us to put on the face of success in public for others to see, while we experience private failures behind closed doors. The Bible tells us that God is "faithful and just to forgive our sins", if we confess them (1 John 1:9). I gained so much victory over the condemnation Satan put upon me by simply confessing my struggles. If you are struggling with secret sins, I encourage you to confess them to a trusted church authority who can help you.

Throughout this journey, the leader in the church whom my aunt connected me with had become as a father to me. He helped me tremendously by talking through many of the questions and challenges I had. He always pointed me to the Word of God. There were times when I needed help but he wasn't available. But because he taught me the value of a relationship with Jesus, I knew that I could call upon the Lord myself and receive the help I needed. We should never develop a dependency upon those whom we receive counsel from. Our dependency should be on the Lord. He is our help in the time of trouble. When no one else is around, God is there. I had to learn that Jesus was even more reliable than those whom I called in my time of need.

There were many things about me that changed as a result of God changing my surroundings. It is almost inevitable for us to pick up habits from those whom we hang around the most. Many of my friends were very effeminate and as a result, I adopted a lot of their ways because I wanted to be just like them. For so long, we called each other 'girl' to the point where I actually believed it. I knew I wasn't a female biologically, but I accepted an identity as a feminine man and acted out as such. It took so long not to see myself as 'one of the girls'. There were some clothes I had in my closet connected to my former identity. Although I was saved, I couldn't comfortably wear certain types of clothing because of how it made me feel and because of who I now represented. I watched myself transform into a man over the years. I couldn't believe what I was seeing in the mirror looking back at me. I was changing. And it didn't happen because I forced myself to wear certain clothing, or speak in a deeper tone of voice, or walk in a certain manner in order to give the impression of masculinity. I would shed tears in disbelief and shock because the person I once was no longer looked back at me. The broken person I had been and was acquainted with was no more. I was emerging more and more into a new creation.

Ron Speaking at A 2020 New Year's Eve Service

Chapter Ten
Am I Really Delivered?

There hath no temptation taken you but such as is common to man: but God is faithful, who will not suffer you to be tempted above that ye are able; but will with the temptation also make a way to escape, that ye may be able to bear it.
1 Corinthians 10:13

Words are a powerful means of communication. Hence, it is important that we provide a Biblical definition for the use of the term 'deliverance'. It has a different meaning for different people and it is tossed around very loosely. There's a belief that one is not fully delivered from homosexuality if they still have same-sex attractions or wrestle with the temptation to act upon desires from their previous life. "If you are really free, you will no longer have a desire for that which you've been delivered from." That's what I've heard. But rather than looking to other people who have been delivered and using their experiences as the norm for everyone else, I think we should look to the scriptures for our hope.

It is clear in the writings of Paul that the born-again believer will be at war against their sin nature for the rest of their lives. Perhaps we may not always battle with the same temptations or have urges to the same degree as we once did, but we will always war against something. It would be grand if our flesh received salvation at the same time our spirit-man did. But sadly, that is not the case. We must contend with, wrestle, and rebuke our own selves, bringing under subjection this body of death to the power of Jesus Christ reigning within us. That includes our thoughts and actions. My pastor often says, "Our flesh is a mess!" Truer words have not been spoken. Our flesh wants what it wants, when it wants it. But through the power of the Holy Ghost, we no longer have to yield to sin. We can say 'No.' Or, we can say 'Yes.' The power of the Spirit gives us the ability to make a decision, and if we choose Him over sin, He equips us to overcome every time.

Every day I am faced with temptation of some kind. I struggled greatly with lust for many years. In part, it was due to the things I did in my past life. But it was also connected with the abuse I endured as a child. I remember sitting at my desk at work years ago. There was a guy whom I found to be quite attractive. I found myself wanting to lust after him. It just so happened that his desk was right in front of mine. But before my mind could wander into a space of lust and get comfortable as it once did, I felt God's presence—convicting me in my conscience. It was as if Jesus was standing behind me so closely that I could feel His breath on the back of my neck.

While the thought of lusting after him was exciting to my flesh, I knew God wouldn't be pleased. I aimed to be as transparent in my conversations with God as much as possible.

I'm often asked what has been helpful most on my journey of walking in freedom. Among many things I could say, prayer is one that tops the list. I felt I had to approach God so mechanically.

> Our Father in heaven, hallowed be your name, your kingdom come, your will be done, on earth as it is in heaven.

Matthew 6:9-13

Not to say that the Lord's prayer is mechanical, but I had to learn how to talk to God like He was truly my friend—like He knew me intimately and I, Him. It went from *The Lord's Prayer* to, "God, I am burning in my flesh and if you don't help me, I may fall into temptation." Rather than being vague, I became specific with God about the who, what, when, where, and why of my temptation. Jesus wasn't intimidated by the realness of my struggles— whether it was in a dream or sitting right in front of me. He wanted me to trust Him with the most vulnerable spaces of my heart, which involved sharing things with Him I wasn't so readily willing to share with others. And in releasing what I was feeling or thinking to Him, He released His power and grace to overcome what I was facing. Get real, and raw with God. He can handle it, and He already knows before you tell Him. He understands the complexities of the human condition (sin) much more than we do. And as we yield to Him and invite Him into our struggles- through prayer, He helps us navigate them. He helped me look the other way and denounce the thoughts of lust toward him in that moment. It's awesome that God doesn't expose what we confide in Him. He's trustworthy. Because He is our refuge, He is a safe place. Have I always chosen Jesus over lusting after someone? No. There have been many times when my flesh was weak and if Jesus had not strengthened me in a moment of temptation, I would have fallen.

Holiness is a daily choice. Remember that. I have learned that even in the moments when we don't think we want to be kept, Jesus is a keeper. When I found myself in vulnerable situations that could have went left, God intervened and helped me before I made the wrong choice. After ten years of walking on this journey of relationship with God, I have not gone back to men. It doesn't mean it was easy, nor does it mean I wasn't presented with someone worthy of my consideration. But God was, is, and will always be faithful. He will not allow you to be tempted above what you are able to handle – and when the temptation comes, He will make a way of escape. That is a promise in the scriptures from God Himself. When the way of escape comes, take it. I had come way too far in my walk with God to allow how I was feeling to cause a ship wreck. Our feelings can be dangerous. That is why our confidence must be in the Lord.

There were many times when I questioned my salvation in light of the fact that I still wrestled with desires for a man. If the people who said true deliverance is measured by whether or not the attractions remain, by their definition, I was not free. I thought I was displeasing God because I still found men attractive. Due to that understanding, I lived in a constant state of anxiety. It was torment actually. However, over time, the attractions to men began to significantly change and decrease. No matter what I did, how much I prayed, fasted, or went to church, the attractions did not leave. It is sufficient to say that God is not pleased when we allow lustful thoughts to take residence in our minds, thereby becoming sin. However, it is not a sin to be tempted. I'd like to say that again. It is not a sin to be tempted. Satan often attacks our minds to condemn us. He tells us, because we still wrestle with attractions, we have not been changed. Deliverance is not the absence of temptation, but it is the power to turn away from the temptation presented to us. One thing is certain, you can't close Pandora's box once you've opened it. While we may no longer have a desire to engage in certain behaviors, we may never forget how it felt to do them or the pleasure we received from them. Our flesh has a memory and it was a daily war conquering thoughts of the promiscuity of my past. Some days were easier than others but nonetheless, it was a fight. I learned that a fight is a good thing because once upon a time, there was no resistance. I thank God that there is a struggle now, a fight now. It tells me that something has changed on the inside of me. Thanks be unto God, I can fight because He has equipped me for the battle. I am grateful to know that I am not fighting alone. God is with me. He is in my thoughts. He is in my heart. However, He can only be in those places if we let Him in. I allowed myself to believe my homosexual temptations were isolated from heterosexual temptations, as something no one could relate to. In conversations with friends who don't experience same-sex attraction, they described their struggle with lust in the same manner as I described my experience. Instantly, the light bulb went off in my head that I was not alone in this fight against the flesh.

Although your sin may not be homosexuality, we all have a sin nature to wrestle with. The remedy is still the same—Jesus. He is the universal solution to humanity's sin problem. That is why His sacrifice on Calvary was once and for all, and for all of mankind. I am encouraged to know that someone, at some point in time, endured my struggle and overcame it with the help of Jesus Christ. There truly is nothing new under the sun. There are no Christians who are void of temptation. God had to reshape my concept of what salvation really was all about. Salvation is not a one and done deal and poof, be gone temptation, be gone memories of every encounter I've ever had. Salvation is the redemption of our soul from God's wrath, which is to come upon those who reject Him and His gospel. We are rescued by Jesus Christ from the death we deserved to die. If we continue in the faith, we have the assurance that we will be saved once and for all in eternity with our blessed Redeemer. That hope assures me that I won't have to wrestle with my sin nature forever. Liberation is coming. That day, temptation will cease. There will be no more sin, and no more tempter. But until then, we have to fight.

In a world progressively promoting sin in media, law, education, and everywhere else, the truth of the gospel remains—anyone can be saved. Jesus Christ, God in the flesh, our great High Priest, was tempted in all points like we are every day, yet He did not yield to sin (Hebrews 4:5). If Jesus was tempted, what makes us think we won't be tempted as well? But just as Jesus was victorious over sin, we can be, too. His power is what makes us strong, not our own human efforts. Going to the gym to become physically fit won't equip you to overcome sin, but becoming spiritually fit in the Spirit will. Although we cannot choose our temptations, we can choose what we will yield to. An analogy I was taught is this: You cannot stop the bird from flying over the tree, but you can prevent it from building a nest. Spiritual application: You cannot stop thoughts from coming to your mind (tree), but you can prevent those thoughts from festering in your mind (building a nest) and becoming sin.

In the moments when I wanted to lust after men, the Holy Spirit would convict me and give me strength to look away and denounce the thought from my mind. Yes, there will be times when we fall short. But know that we can repent and continue in the race. A fall doesn't have to become a bed that we lay in and stay in. We can get back up again. Accountability was vital for me. The daily conversations I had with the leader from my church were extremely helpful for me through my journey. I had so many questions about temptation, the Christian journey, and just faith in general. Having conversations with him gave me an opportunity to make sense of some of the thoughts in my mind and find answers to thoughts in the Word of God.

The world suggests 'What I feel, therefore, I am.' For the Christian, our temptations and feelings do not define us. More specifically, sexual attraction is not what defines the believer. The death, burial, and resurrection of Jesus Christ does. The old man is buried with Christ in baptism and we arise to walk in the newness of life—in a new identity. That means I am brand-spanking new. Jesus took me out of a box and introduced me to the world. Not used, but as new. Not tarnished, but clean. I'm completely made over. Once I developed an understanding that my temptations don't define me, I was able to walk confidently in my identity as a son of God, as a man. It gave validation of the truths of the scripture. It made my Christian walk more bearable. Suddenly, I no longer questioned my salvation; I affirmed it.

I just wanted so badly to be changed. I wanted to be able to wake up one morning and have none of my feminine mannerisms. I didn't want to look in the mirror and be reminded of my past. But as much as I was in a hurry, God wasn't. He wanted to walk me through His transforming power day-by-day. I remember many times when I'd sit in a room of masculine, heterosexual men and have silent anxiety attacks because I felt inadequate in comparison to them. Perhaps it was the bass in their voices, the way in which they walked and talked—their machismo. Nothing about them said femininity. I wanted that. I was chasing after an ideal of masculinity or manhood that God never told me I needed to have.

Sometimes we worry too much about changing ourselves, which leads to anxiety and frustration with ourselves and God. I learned that the change takes place when we stop trying to do God's job. We can't change ourselves. Our focus must be on loving Jesus, yielding to Him, and allowing Him to do the changing. We can go great lengths to change the outer appearance but if our hearts are still the same, then we haven't changed where it matters most. We must surrender ourselves totally to God. What do I mean by total surrender? In short, we must be willing to give God our whole self—our attractions, our wants, desires, ideals about ourselves, our mind and heart, our fears, our will. Everything. We will not see true deliverance without truly surrendering. Deliverance must come on God's terms, not our own.

I am often reminded that God is the potter and we are the clay. Let the potter shape us, mold us, and make us however He pleases. My critical focus on Ron's ideas of masculinity robbed me of so much joy in being in relationship with the Creator of heaven and earth. I had missed the purpose of relationship completely. My brother, my sister, I admonish you to stop trying to change yourself and focus on building a relationship with Jesus. Relationship allowed me to hear what God's thoughts were of me, although my thoughts of myself were not good. I needed to hear Him tell me He loved me though I wasn't where I wanted to be, or that His love for me was not contingent on anything I could do or attempted to do in efforts of changing myself. As my mind began to transform through the understanding of God's expectations of me, it began to feel less like religion and more like a father-son relationship. Many people walk away from God because they don't see the kind of change they expect, or when they expect it. Sometimes our healing or change isn't expedient. It's a process that must be walked through with godly counsel, relationship with believers, and submission to God.

In Luke 17, there were nine lepers whom Jesus had cleansed. After their cleansing, Jesus told them to go and show themselves to the priest. Verse 14 says, "as they went, they were cleansed."

I'd like you to consider the fact that their healing didn't take place until they started walking. As you continue on this journey with God, know that you are being healed each day in ways you probably cannot see in the moment. People at my church would often comment on just how much I was changing before their eyes. Sometimes, I couldn't see what they were talking about. But it was in my walk with God. Sometimes He allows others to see the things we cannot see in order to encourage us. Yes, there was an outward change that was visible. However, more pronounced was what I saw when I looked into the windows of my soul through my eyes. I saw strength looking back at me. I saw self-love. I saw power and authority. I saw godliness. I saw growth. I saw tenacity. I saw a man of God. I once lusted after men for qualities or characteristics they had which I perceived I did not have. As God began to reveal to me the man I was created to be in Him and when I began to walk in that, I no longer lusted after men in the same ways anymore. Who I was and who I was becoming was the man God saw in me all along. The Lord wanted me to look to Him to understand my identity as a man—not to society, not to pop culture, but to Him. There was a purging I went through of myself to become more like Him. I was being emptied of everything I thought I was. At times, it felt like I was having separation anxiety. I had changed in so many ways that I didn't recognize myself anymore. It was definitely intimidating, but I trusted that the direction God had for my life was worth pursuing, even if the Ronald of tomorrow looked nothing like the Ronald of today. It would be complete surrender. I remember bagging up the majority of my closet to give away my clothes. It was very hard to see myself as a new creature when I still wore the same clothes I had in my previous life. I no longer felt comfortable in some of the clothes I used to wear.

This was a huge leap of faith. I barely had any money at the time to restock my wardrobe, but I trusted God to restore everything because I took a step of faith to please Him. For awhile, I repeated some of the same outfits. No one told me to change how I was dressing. This was something God dealt with my heart about. The husband of the woman I met in Target was one of the deacons in the church, and she offered to take me shopping to purchase two new suits. Not long after, others began to bless me with clothes. I took out my studded ear rings and discarded them. I was willing to surrender whatever God asked of me and what my pastor asked of me, without a fight. God intended for the new me to be reflective of Him on the inside and in my outward appearance.

Something incredible was happening in me. As I mentioned before, I had lost all attraction for women when I was in *the life,* but somewhere along this journey, He began to restore to me the natural affections of a man. I found myself desirous of being with a woman. The desire for marriage was still in my heart. I didn't want to be married to prove my salvation or my deliverance. I wanted a family. I wanted someone to love and cherish in a committed, life-long marriage. I wanted the *American Dream* from chapter one, still. I said to God, "If marriage is in Your will for me, I want a wife who can empathize with my past".

I asked for someone who would love me and not be uncomfortable with my truth. Someone who would complement the ministry God had called me to. And then I started to get meticulous – I asked for a woman with long beautiful hair. If she had short hair, I knew she wasn't the one. So I continued narrowing down a list, not knowing that I was describing Fetima.

Fetima and Ron

Chapter Eleven
Gideon

I remember sitting in our Young Adult Sunday School class as the Sunday School teacher was teaching on the story of Gideon from the book of Judges. He was talking about the importance of obedience to God. He said,

"God isn't talking to everyone so it would behoove you to listen when He speaks!"

From the lesson, a question was posed to the class. Among the many responses, I heard a voice I wasn't familiar with. It was soft. It was sassy. It was pretty, hee-hee. It caught my attention. My spidey senses were tingling and I just had to know, *who was this woman?* I didn't want to be obvious and look back, but I was captivated by the articulation of her response. I found an excuse to turn back and glance at the face of the woman whose words were so wise. 'She's beautiful', I thought to myself and smiled. At the end of Sunday School, I heard the voice of God say to me,

"Tell her I have a plan for her life and if she follows me, I will show her what it is."

I started responding to God in my mind, asking if this was really Him speaking to me or if this was my own thought. I didn't want to be one of those "God told me to tell you . . ." *prophets*, prophesying lies. He affirmed His instruction to me, and I obediently went to her after Sunday School concluded. I remember this moment like it was yesterday.

I said, "I know we don't know each other and this may sound strange, but God told me to tell you He has a plan for your life and that if you follow Him, He will show you what it is."

She responded, "Actually, I do know you. We went to high school together."

She introduced herself as Fetima, and we shook hands. Following her formal introduction, she told me God had been speaking to her for years telling her He had a work for her to do, but she always told Him she wasn't ready. With a look of shock, she said,

"This is confirmation that the same God who speaks to me is the same God speaking to everyone else."

I thought, 'Whew. So, I'm not a false prophet?!' There was an interesting connection between us in that moment. At least it was for me. Perhaps I should ask her if she felt it too. From there, we spoke to each other often when we saw one another at church. She was so bright-eyed and bushy-tailed when she saw me. 'This girl must like me', I thought to myself. I mean, I can't blame her. Anyway, what gave her away the most was when I caught her staring at me from a distance in the back of the church while I was up front. I waved to her and she came down towards the front where I was. There was this awkward tension between us and as a knee-jerk reaction, she gave me a high five. We burst into laughter, and she walked away. We later exchanged Google Chat names with the intention to get to know one another more. We talked all day long at work. Her comedic personality made me smile, and the laughs were endless. As time progressed, we began pouring our lives out to one another. I mean deep stuff. It was then that I learned she was once a lesbian and bi-sexual for nine years. It was always harder to discern women who came out of *the life* than men for me. Apparently, we had the same friend groups in high school who were also gay, yet we never knew one another. I was two classes ahead of her. I graduated in 2006 and she graduated in 2008. I could relate to this girl down to the most minuscule details of our lives. We opened up about our experiences with sexual abuse and rape. The molestation we endured as children was even inflicted by the same relative to us. I was a bit in awe. She said to me,

> "I've told you more about my life than anyone else I know. Even my closest friends don't know some of the stuff you know. If this doesn't go anywhere, I might have to kill you!"

We laughed hysterically, which was evidenced by the multiple LOLs we exchanged. This was something special. A special friendship? Very possible. I didn't know with certainty, but I did know we shared something very unique.

Our friendship blossomed over time. We hung out together innocently. At some point, it was pretty evident that there was a spark between us. I developed romantic feelings toward her and I wanted to know if this relationship had the potential to become something lifelong. Although I had a wall up, 'Full-fledged Fetima'—as she called herself—was tearing down that wall. My mind went back to the prayer I prayed pertaining to a wife. Fetima met the description of literally everything I prayed for, except the hair. Her hair was

Ron and Fetima

struggling a bit on hang time. 'Well, she's not the one!', I jokingly said to myself. *Could this be the one?* I had literally bared my whole life to this woman, and she wasn't intimidated by my past, just as I wasn't intimidated by hers. I had some scars and some baggage, and so did she. As I continued to seek God in prayer, He revealed that Fetima was supposed to be my wife. He proved it to me in ways I couldn't have imagined. In particular, through my insecurities.

We started dating officially and had become public with our relationship. One day, we went shopping in Virginia at Tyson's Corner Mall. We were walking in the mall, holding hands, and I began to have an anxiety attack. In that moment, it felt like everyone was looking at us, wondering what Fetima was doing holding the hand of this gay man. I was trembling and trying to hide it in my body language. I constantly wrestled with my masculinity. I still saw characteristics of a woman in me. Although I had come a long way in my new life, the opinions of other people weighed heavily on me. I feared that people on the outside would not see the change from the inside and would subsequently judge me and us based on my outward appearance. I cried and poured out my heart to her after we left. I felt so inadequate and unsure of myself. I questioned whether or not I could do this relationship and be the man she needed. The insecurities lived in my head, but they weren't a concern in hers.

I didn't want her to see this side of me. I would have much rather dealt with that by myself when I got home. This opportunity allowed me to see just how much I needed her and one of the reasons why God chose her for me. She spoke life into me. She reminded me that she loves Ronald McCray for who he is. She wasn't concerned about what people may have thought about us. She affirmed me. She affirmed us. She affirmed the man I struggled to see within myself. She spoke to the leader in me before I even saw myself as one. Even in a moment of fragility, she was able to see strength. She was able to see what God was making me into, even when I couldn't see it myself. Every man or woman should marry someone to whom they can bare their all to without fear of judgment. She gave me the balance I needed, and I gave the same to her. Although polar opposites in some respects, we were jointly fit together, perfectly.

There were some churchgoers who questioned her decision to be with me. I heard the stories of men who abandoned their families to be with other men. Perhaps I was being viewed from the lens of other people's experiences. I found this projection to be as equally unfair as it was understandable. There were even people whom I highly respected that hurt me with their words behind my back by trying to convince Fetima why being with me was a bad idea all because of who I used to be. I honestly wanted to leave the church and never come back. I didn't want to leave church in general, but I wanted to leave this specific church. However, God wouldn't let me. He made me develop character in the bitter soil He had planted me in. If I was going to preach His gospel of salvation and deliverance, I had to be able to endure mockery, scorn, lies, and deceit. I had to be able to endure people who smiled in my face but talked about me behind my back. Jesus endured it before I did, so I knew I could overcome.

One of the most difficult experiences in my Christian journey has been being a male in the African-American church who turned away from the practice of homosexuality. It probably would've been easier to hide my past if I didn't look like where I came from. That is to say, I used to fit the description of a stereotypical gay man. In the African-American church, being gay is like the cardinal sin. At the top of the pyramid is homosexuality and underneath falls every other sin. Sometimes, I don't think the Church actually believes what it preaches. We quote scriptures like Jeremiah 32:27 and Matthew 19:26 when it comes to everything else under the sun. But when it comes to *this* sin, we don't believe the Word can change people. If we did, we wouldn't treat gay people the way in which we do. II Corinthians 5:17 reminds us that:

> If any man be in Christ, he is a new creature: old things are passed away; behold, all things are become new.

As difficult as that period of my life was, I thank God He took me through it, because today I am stronger. I am more confident in my identity as a man and a son of God than I have ever been. The enemy can no longer use the opinions of others to stop me from walking confidently in who I am. It meant a lot for my now wife to stand on what God told her to do, which is to marry me in spite of what others may have thought. I had confidence that she would be my ride or die partner. We were a team, a force to be reckoned with in Jesus. But my insecurities led to a two-week break up. No one knew about it, except for the few people whom we trusted. But God brought us back together to fulfill His will for our lives.

We joined together in holy matrimony on November 7th, 2015 on a beautiful, rainy day at our church. My life changed forever. As I looked into her eyes before we kissed at the altar, I saw God's goodness and His faithfulness looking back at me. He heard every word I prayed to Him that day. He went beyond the things I could think of to pray for. He gave me things I needed in a wife that I would have never thought to ask for. Not only did He hear that prayer, but He heard the silent desires of my heart in Chapter One, when I sat in the room among friends. When we said, "I do," God proved to me—and to the devil—that all things are possible with God.

If you would have told me I'd ever be married to a woman when I first gave my life to Christ back in

Ron and Fetima's Wedding Day

2009, I would have laughed at you. He proved to me that homosexuality is not an impossibility. He was making all things new in me. I have a wife whom I can trust with my life. We don't keep secrets from each other. We can openly share our temptations and struggles with each other and pray for one another. When I am being attacked by the enemy, she anoints my head with oil, lays hands on me, and prays over me—and I do the same for her. I have never found a love quite like this in another human being. I thought I knew love in the relationships I had with men, but how can you know true love except God be in the midst of it? This spiritual union connected our spirits and our hearts together as one. I went from learning to be a man, to learning to be a husband. The journey of being a godly husband may very well be another book. Fetima and I have the privilege of sharing the gospel together as we are living witnesses of what the power of God can do. I'd like to say that marriage is not the goal of the person who comes out of the LGBT+ lifestyle. Loving Jesus and being in relationship with Him is. Before I had my girl, I had Jesus. Now I have Jesus and my wife. And if God be for us, who can be against us? The plans God spoke of for my wife, through me, was the work He has us doing together now. It amazes me how detailed God is—that He would take two people from very similar backgrounds, who share many of the same experiences, and bring them together for His glory. We shared the same friend groups in high school and some in middle school, but we never met one another. She was raised a few blocks from where I was raised. God had my wife in my vicinity for the majority of my life but never allowed me to meet her until ten years after we graduated from high school. She told me as I walked past her in the hallway once during my senior year, a voice spoke to her saying, "He is going to be your husband." At the time, we were both in the life. Perhaps this voice was mistaken. But a decade later, the prophecy was fulfilled.

Chapter Twelve
The Marvelous Light

I started writing my story about nine years ago. I began writing from a perspective that I didn't have today. As of October 18th, 2019, I had walked with God for ten years. **I've searched the scriptures, and through the period of time I've walked with God, I have found Him to be everything He says He is in His Word.** Not only has Jesus redeemed my soul, but He has given me new life. He has given me a life I never imagined possible. I used to think God doesn't hear the prayers of sinners. That was until He answered the prayers I prayed years before I ever knew Him as my Lord and Savior. Every morning I wake up next to my wife, I remember God's faithfulness and kindness to me. I will never understand why He chose me. Of all the things I did in rebellion to Him, He still wanted me. I am not deserving of this life. I didn't know what it was to have joy until I came to know Christ. I am no longer overcome with depression and brokenness, and my heart is no longer heavy in despair. I don't desire to take my own life anymore. I walk in a freedom I didn't know I could have. I am alive in Christ! I often hear the LGBT+ community accuse those who no longer identify as gay as sad, depressed people, because they are denying themselves. I can say that denying myself for the sake of knowing Christ has brought me joy and fulfillment that I was never able to find in my life as a gay man. In denying myself, God has given me more of Himself. I couldn't find joy living my life without God. Society says people who formerly identified as LGBT+ don't exist. I'm one witness of many proclaiming that we do exist! If I had not given my life to Jesus, I would have missed out on life as a husband, and a father.

Our son, Alexander, was born February 25th,

Ron, Fetima, and Alexander's First Christmas
Photo By MFieldsphotography

2019. Oh, how our lives have changed since this little guy came and turned our world upside down. Sometimes, this all feels like a dream. I went through what felt like hell in my life, to now living a life of so much joy. And if this is a dream, please let me sleep! Why is the light of Christ so marvelous? Because when you've lived in darkness, that's all you know. The splendor of His light and love pierced through the shadows I once lived in and has illuminated a new path for me to walk upon.

Had the Church affirmed my homosexual identity and told me God was okay with it, I would have missed everything God had for me. I would have never been the father of Alexander or the husband to Fetima. I would have never known the transforming power of Jesus Christ. I wouldn't have a testimony to tell anyone about God. We will never know the transforming power of Jesus until we die to ourselves because the beginning of loving Jesus is death to who we are. I had traveled down a dark tunnel for the majority of my life, unable to see the light at the end of it. I walked aimlessly hoping for the day where I would be lifted from the pit of destruction Satan had dug for me. Now I can tell the world that my Redeemer lives! I know because He lives in me. I no longer live under the shadows of other people's opinions. I know who I am and no one can take that away from me.

Chapter Thirteen
Dear, BFF

On December 9th, 2010, I wrote and dedicated a letter to my BFF who died in 2009. When my best friend died, my life changed dramatically. I aimed to re-create the letter just as I wrote it nine years ago.

Dear former BFF,

It's been a long time coming pal! We have been best friends forever or BFFs for as long as I can recall in my own thoughts. You got me into so much trouble coming up, *lol*. I remember the time you introduced me to the club, or the first time I found out what liquor tasted like. When I consumed too much of it, I lost cognizance of where I was and you influenced me to let go and "live a little." You opened my eyes to what the world was all about and all I had to gain, but never told me what I had to lose. Life in the fast lane, or on the edge, was where the in-crowd usually hung out, and you made me believe that I should follow them. So of course, I did. You always knew how to get the best of me and how to get me to do what you wanted me to do.

You even made me disobey my parents, lie to people, and trick myself into thinking I was actually making myself happy. I remember growing up in church, but for some reason you never wanted me to go and it began to always be about you. From that point, I guess those sweet nothings you whispered really convinced me to trust you and be at your command. You opened my eyes to all that I *thought* I was missing! And honestly, sometimes I really did have fun! But what I didn't see was the path of destruction you were taking me down, or how your motive since I was born was to kill me. All along it's really been about you and not me. Man, was I so blind?! Love is truly blind, because you had me walking around with my eyes shut thinking I was moving in the right direction. I was so used to being abused and battered down I guess. The only love I experienced or knew to be true was the love I thought I received from you. It was such a dog eat dog world, and it was so dark, like I was lost in a tunnel. I remember the nights I cried when I got tired of holding your hand and doing whatever you told me to do. I wanted OUT. I just didn't know how to end such a long-term committed relationship with you. But that day, when I was walking through the tunnel in the darkness, a familiar voice spoke to me. I knew the voice, I just couldn't put a finger on who it was. I heard the voice, but I saw no one. It said to me, "I love you. Take my hand, I will lead the way." I thought to myself 'I must be going crazy!' And I remember I was a little reluctant, because I guess I didn't believe I could be shown another way. For months, that voice was always there and helped me see outside of what you always told me I needed to do to be happy.

He said to me, "I've been here all along, but you decided not to hear me." Then He said. "I've been out here knocking all this time, but you never let Me in. I almost gave up on you, but My love wouldn't allow me to do it. Because I knew your heart, I was willing to wait, even when My hand was out for you and you turned away and spit in My face."

I began to really evaluate what really was taking place in my life, and where I was headed if I continued down that dark road. I began to speak back to the voice, and it led me to a place of comfort and expectancy of joy. I actually found myself interested. It was like the voice that came to me used a man to speak to me, as well as hundreds of other sick and wounded people in this building with beautiful music and kind souls. This place was familiar, I just hadn't been in what felt like ages. It felt like home. I had flashbacks of this place. The words that were said to me were with me from childhood until the time I sat in that seat as an adult. After months of this therapy, I was offered a petition by the voice through that man yet again. It was almost like the man knew my whole life, but we had never spoken before. The voice told me that if I came with Him, He would be all I need, and He would make sure I never had to worry or be afraid again. It sounded too good to be true, but He said, "If only you believe, I will do just what I said."

So, I did it! I took Him at His word and the same voice that spoke to me also spoke through me. I tried to control my tongue and reformulate my words to make sense of them, but I lost utter control and was taken to a place I had never been before. My body felt numb and I felt a heavenly presence come over me. I thought I was going to float from where I kneeled. I cried aloud with my hands in the air saying something I couldn't recognize, but it just felt so good. And ever since that day, I've had that voice with me and it has guided me and gave me liberation from you, my BFF.

I have been able to overcome you, even when you rose up and mocked me. When you tempted me, I was able to say, "NO!" This is something I couldn't have done before, no matter how many times I had tried. I realized then how empowered I was, and that my BFF had been replaced with a new friend, comforter, regulator, companion, and emperor. This new feeling was amazing! Sometimes, when the sun would rise early in the morning, I would lay in silence with tears of amazement. I couldn't believe where I was or who I had become. I feel like I've been taken out of a box, unwrapped, and introduced as brand new. It's not a show I put on, it's not something I have to try so hard to do—this is who I am! I guess that's the amazing part, because I remember He told me that with Him all things would be possible. He proved that through my life and worked a miracle. No one will ever know some of the hidden chapters of my life but Him. And no, I'm not ashamed of where I came from because He told me everyone started in the same state. It was just the outward expressions of what was in them already that were manifested differently. He helped me realize the importance of only being concerned with what He had to think of me.

Man, I love Him so much! I feel so complete! I had been walking with this person all this time and I asked,

"What is your name?" He said to me "I AM."
From the day of my new birth, He has been that I AM in my life. He is keeping me and I won't turn my back on Him! He has been so, so good! I finally made it to the end of the tunnel! And now I can see! I thank God for the Holy Ghost that awakened this dead spirit in me, and put my BFF—my flesh—to rest.

> Therefore if any man [be] in Christ, [he is] a new creature: old things are passed away; behold, all things are become new. 2 Corinthians 5:17

Chapter Fourteen
Is God Who He Says He Is?

Fetima and Ron

During a very transparent conversation I had with a leader of my church, I was told that not many pastors and leaders believe gay people can be delivered. Although this was not the first time I'd heard this, the impact was the same each time those words were uttered. My heart became heavy and my eyes welled with tears. I wanted to cry for every person who would desire freedom from homosexuality but would find no help from certain churches. I wanted to cry for every parent praying for their gay son or daughter to find the hope that is in Jesus Christ, which leads to a conversion of the heart and a change in one's life. Moreover, my heart cried for the Church who proclaims freedom for some, but not for all. Our disbelief sends the message that perhaps Jesus was mistaken about His power and ability. It sends the message that there is power in the gospel to save and bring change to the lives of everyone, minus the LGBT+ community. It occurred to me that if we don't believe the gospel has the power to save and deliver all, then how can we, as the Church, expect the world and those struggling with same-sex attraction to believe it? I believe the root of the issue here is not that we don't have faith that gay people can change, but rather, it is our lack of faith in God. We have become as gods, supposing that our experienced-based opinions supersede the authority of God's Word—to which, we must repent.

I want to admonish those who identify within the Church—whether affirming or not—and to believe God is exactly who He says He is in the scriptures. Perhaps you don't have examples sitting in your pews of those who are walking in freedom from homosexuality. Maybe you've seen some start off well, but somehow have turned back to their old lifestyle. Our faith isn't hinged upon isolated examples of men and women. It's hinged upon the resurrection of Jesus Christ. If He didn't rise from the dead on the third day, we are all wasting our time with a religion whose hope will end in the grave. But we have hope, because Jesus is risen from the dead. Our hope is that the same power which raised Christ from the dead will also quicken our mortal bodies when the Lord returns for His Church. But in the here and now, we must submit our hearts to God, whose power can transform the life of anyone who puts their faith in Him. There is no other hope outside of the gospel. Hebrews 13:8 reminds us that Jesus Christ is the same yesterday, today, and forever. He has not changed. This gospel brings the hope of new life to every soul stained with sin. On October 18th, 2009, I found that great hope when Jesus filled me with His Holy Spirit and changed my life.

My story is just one example of a LGBT+-identified person whom Christ has changed. Since sharing my story, I have connected with former gay, lesbian, transgender, and bi-sexual people from around the world whom Jesus has changed. There are many of us. God is raising up an army of men and women who are not afraid to proclaim their freedom to the world—and even some churches—who have denied His identity and His power. I have spoken to people around the world who do not want to be gay anymore, yet because of fear of judgment from their church leadership, congregations, and families, they silently struggle in sin. Then they are judged when they return to their former identities. Our churches must be a safe space for any and every one to bring their struggles and find support in a loving, trusted environment. Although there are many who do not desire change, there are many who do. Our arms and the doors of the Church should be open to those hungry souls.

For a moment, I'd like us to consider the unnamed leper who met Jesus in the first chapter of Gospel of Mark. Whether we know it or not, all of us were that leper—whether gay, straight, black, white, rich, or poor. We have all sinned and fallen short of God's glory. But Jesus, being moved with compassion, reached out and touched the leper and cleansed him. Jesus extended His hand of compassion toward humanity when He gave His life for us on the cross, and shed His blood to reconcile us back into relationship with Him. We were all destined for eternity separated from God. Yet, He loved us so much that He gave His only Son, that whoever would believe on Him would not perish, but have everlasting life (John 3:16). That means there is hope for absolutely anyone who is living and breathing.

I have searched the scriptures about this Jesus of Nazareth and I have come to the conclusion that He is everything He says He is. He is hope for the hopeless, for He gives new life. He is water for the thirsty, and food for the hungry. He is the Savior of the world, the awaited Messiah, and the King of the world. He is God, the Creator of heaven and Earth. He is the Prince of Peace, and the One by whom we know true joy. In His hand, He satisfies the desire of every living thing (Psalm 145:16). He has truly satisfied the desire of my soul and can do the same for everyone who surrenders their life to Him. Is God who He says He is? Can God change someone's life? Can God mend a heart that is broken? You be the judge.

God's Plan of Salvation

The death, burial, and resurrection of Jesus Christ is perhaps the most compelling love story in the existence of humanity. Jesus was beaten mercilessly, spat upon, crucified on a cross, and pierced in His side with a spear. He gave His life to redeem us from the penalty of sin and to reconcile us back unto Himself. God Himself, manifested in the person of Jesus Christ (Colossians 2:9), became our sacrifice and died the death we deserved for our sins. As a result of His sacrifice, we now have a divine privilege to accept His invitation of redemption, and to live eternally with Him. Jesus said we must be born again of water and Spirit (John 3:1-7). The Apostle Peter tells us how we can be born again of water and Spirit in the book of Acts, 2:38:

> Then Peter said unto them, **Repent**, and **be baptized every one of you in the name of Jesus Christ** for the remission of sins, and ye shall **receive the gift of the Holy Ghost.**

Please contact me at: McCrayfamilyministry@gmail.com if you have not had this experience. I would love to connect you with a ministry nearest you.

Resources

Books:

Eternal Victim, Eternal Victor. By Donnie McClurkin.

Touching a Dead Man. By Darryl L. Foster.

Gay Girl, Good God. By Jackie Hill-Perry.

Websites:

All Things New (www.allthingsnewlifetransformation.org)

Coming Out Inc. (www.comingoutglobal.com)

Equipped to Love (www.equippedtolove.com)

Freedom March (www.freedomtomarch.com)

His Wonderful Works (https://hiswonderfulworks.com)

My website (www.ronaldjmccray.com)

RAINN Rape, Abuse & Incest National Network)
   (https://www.rainn.org/statistics/victims-sexual-violence)

Restored Hope Network
   (https://www.restoredhopenetwork.org)

Endorsements

"IS GOD Who He Say's He Is?' **will captivate your heart**. *Interwoven throughout the story are examples of God's loving kindness and mercy. If you believe you have gone too far to be saved, that you are beyond hope, read Ron's testimony. Ron can testify that a great change has taken place in his life, and yes God Is Who He Say He Is!"*
– **Bishop Charles E. Johnson, Senior Pastor, Greater Morning Star Apostolic Ministries**

"As a parent who has a child with SSA, **Ronald McCray fanned the flame of Hope**. *His struggles and victories gave me more in-depth insight and greater compassion, along with equipping me to go the distance in prayer and fight for the freedom of my child."*
– **Melinda Patrick, Director of Parent Support for His Wonderful Works, Inc. and Founder of Hope Community**

"Reading this autobiography was as compelling as watching a movie. **I would recommend this book to parents, family and friends of an LGBT+ loved one, as well as anyone battling with same-sex attraction themselves, yet desiring to know if deliverance is possible—especially those that were raised in the church and have somehow drifted away.** *Ronald's story is full of real life truth, vulnerability and compassion; naturally provoking and challenging the reader to want to confront the pain of their past. The title poses a question to its audience, "Is God Who He Says He Is?" After reading this book, my response is, 'You Bet!'"* – **Tamika C. Sanders, Founder/Executive Director Coming Out, Inc.**

"Is God Who He Says He Is?', *is a book that* **will change your perspective on how God can step in and change any situation, no matter how big or small.** *Thank you Ronald McCray for having the courage to share your story of total transformation. This is a must*

READ!!!! – **Terrell L. Sarver, President of BeMen Inc. "Where Every Man Has A Voice"**

"My friend, Ronald McCray, is a walking, talking testimony and trophy of grace. In his riveting book, 'Is God Who He Says He Is?' **he unpacks with both passion and precision God's redemptive power**. Ronald knows firsthand the privilege and peace that comes with grace, second chance and U-Turns. Sadly our culture has bought the lie that pleasing self and 'you do you" leads to the road of fulfillment and happiness but ultimately leads to a dead end. The song "My Way" is the national anthem of Hell, but when we graduate from Satan and society's lies we finally experience the freedom found only in the Gospel Truth.

Over the years, I also searched about God in my own journey, and some said He was a liar, others a lunatic, but **like Ronald, we found God to be Lord**. He embodies Truth and grace, has a Face and His name is Jesus. This book is not only timely but truthful, and **Ronald's story isn't just a game changer but a life changer.** Buy one for your self and four more to give to friends because in a world of hype this brother found Hope and you can too!" - **Frank Shelton, Jr. Author of "Carrying Greatness" & "Blessedness of Brokenness." Former DC/MD/DE State Coordinator @ Billy Graham Evangelistic Assoc. International Evangelism Chairman 2012, 2016 & 2020 Olympics outreach.**

"It's with high honor and deep sincerity that I lend my endorsement to Ronald McCray's book 'Is God Who He Says He Is?' If I could describe it, it would be like having a front row seat at one man's life, death and resurrection event. The highs and the lows of Ron's life are laid bare, but **what shines through is the brilliant love of Jesus, the incomparable power of Jesus and the deep compassion of Jesus.** Ron's incredible ability to convey in contemporary stylings his story and yet root it in the succession of our common salvation experience makes this book altogether unique and mesmerizing." - **Pastor DL Foster, Founder and President Emeritus,**

The Overcomers Network; Author, Touching A Dead Man: One man's explosive story of deliverance from homosexuality

"Ron's testimony in 'Is God Who He Says He Is demonstrates just how patient God is and how relentlessly He pursues His wayward children. This story of vulnerability and transparency is a beacon of hope for anyone who has strayed from God and for any person who is praying for a loved one who has drifted away from God. As God pursued him, Ron experienced first-hand the width and length and depth and height of the love of Jesus Christ and it radically transformed his life! - **Debora Barr, Minister and Author** **www.DBarrMinistries.org**

About the Author

Ronald J. McCray formerly identified as gay for six years. He was born again on October 18th, 2009, according to Acts 2:38 and began to walk out his journey of freedom from homosexuality. He is a writer, speaker, and radio personality whose work and testimony has been featured on *The Christian Post*, *The 700 Club*, *CBN News*, *Charisma News*, *ABC 6 News*, "Here's My Heart: A Documentary of Surrendering to Freedom", Freedom March, *God Reports*, *The Greater Love* and other media outlets around the world. Ronald co-hosts *Transformed Life Radio* with his wife, Fetima, and they are the proud parents of their son, Alexander.

Ronald shares the message of the gospel through sharing his testimony, teaching, preaching and blogging.

Website: www.ronaldjmccray.com.
E-mail: McCrayfamilyministry@gmail.com
Instagram: Iamronjmccray
Facebook: Ronald J. McCray

About the Publisher

At **the Vision to Fruition Publishing House**, we are dedicated to helping others bring their personal, business, ministry and other visions to fruition.

Whether it's as grand as a book you want to write, a business you want to start, a conference or event you want to host, a ministry you want to launch or an organization you want to start; or as small as needing a computer repair, logo design or web design; **The Vision to Fruition Publishing House** is the publishing branch of **the Vision to Fruition Group**. We will help you walk through the process and set you up for success! At **the Vision to Fruition Group** we don't have clients, we have *Visionaries*. We provide solutions to equip others to pursue their visions and dreams with reckless abandon.

In 2018 we published twenty-three authors, eight of which were Amazon Bestsellers. We would love for you to join our family of Visionaries as well!

Learn more here: **www.vision-fruition.com**

Made in the USA
Columbia, SC
07 August 2020